Celebrity Talker

Celebrity sTalker

Stories From a Woman Who Thinks Celebrities Are Dying to Talk to Her. Only They Aren't.

Suzy Soro

Copyright © 2012 by Suzy Soro

All rights reserved. No part of this book may be used or reproduced in any manner whatsoever without written permission, except in the case of brief quotations embodied in critical articles or reviews.
All photos from Suzy Soro's personal collection.
Published 2012 by HumorOutcasts Press
Printed in the United States of America

ISBN 0-615-74132-0
EAN-13 978-061574132-1

For my mom, Olga

Because I'll never be able to repay all the money I owe you.

To my sister Lindy for sharing the best parts of my life. Thank you for never suggesting I get a real job. Without you this book would be a lot shorter. A lot of people may track you down and punish you for that.

To my best friend, Dennison Samaroo, for always believing in me and red wine.

To Donna Cavanagh for her unwavering support. Every writer should know what that feels like. And if you haven't found it yet, keep looking.

To Ed Cavanagh for his spectacularly creative artwork.

To Kirsten Janene-Nelson for her insightful editing and friendship. I'm afraid to type without her.

To Ann Imig for talking me into joining Twitter. I apologize for calling it stupid.

I am forever indebted to the following people for helping me along the incredibly bumpy way:

Burt Levitt, Paul Herzig, Silver Friedman, Mary Hart, Joy Behar, Angela Scott, OmniPop, Leslie Norris Townsend, Rondell Sheridan, Jann Rowe, Jillian Bennett, Amy Bernard-Herman, Henriette Mantel, Dr. Nancy Berk, Larry David, Michael Patrick King, Carol Leifer, Gary LeMel, Linda Smith, Esq., Toni Naples, Lori Tartol, Earl Martin, Steve Gelder, Funny Not Slutty, Ross Cavins, BlogHer, Neal Mayhem, Karla Telega, Lin Robinson, Laurenne Sala, Rahul Subramanian, Corey Podell, and Barry Long.

And finally, to my dad who, were he still alive, would buy one thousand copies of this book and sell them to his friends at the St. Petersburg Yacht Club for twice the cover price.

The Introduction, the Foreword, or the Prologue, Take Your Pick

I'm not a celebrity stalker. Far from it. I have commitment issues, and you need a certain level of that to get entwined with a stranger's life to the extent that you make their existence more important than your own. So, follow a celebrity from a supermarket, try to break into their homes or repeatedly show up at their movie premieres? Too much work. I have to leave Post-it notes on my bathroom mirror to remind myself to put on a bra. Someone hateful bought me a plant for my last birthday and I deleted their number from my gmail contacts. I only buy flowers because I know they die in four days. I refuse to get married because ohmygod is he still *here*?

And yet leaving my apartment involves all the activities that exhaust me. Showering, getting dressed, being polite. So when I finally walk out my front door I'm like a dog whose master has been gone all day and then returns to take me out for a walk. I'm disproportionately excited. I jump on the people who don't want to be jumped on. I immediately turn into a mental patient, and not the good kind that are sedated and in restraints. I can't stop myself. It's harder than when I gave up cigarettes and that cost me two years and a twenty-pound weight gain. For me, talking to celebrities is like a heroin addiction - the urge kicks in and suddenly I'm tying off and shooting up inane conversation. Half of them are pleasant and the other half can hardly wait for me to walk away. Okay, probably all of them can hardly wait for that. So, a celebrity stalker? No. But a celebrity talker? Most definitely.

If I ever get arrested for a murderous spree my neighbors will undoubtedly tell the six o'clock eyewitness news team that I appeared to be "a quiet loner who kept to herself." But joke's on them and the news team because most people don't run up to celebrities and engage them in conversation as if they'd known them forever. Most people can take a hint when a celebrity backs up two feet and clutches their wallet and newborn when you approach them. Most people understand boundaries. I'm not most people. Apparently.

A few years ago a friend insisted I accompany her while she drove by singer Natasha Bedingfield's house in the Hollywood Hills. Seemed innocent enough until my friend asked me what I thought of Natasha's living room couch and I noticed she was holding up a pair of binoculars while we drove by.

"Are you stalking her?"

"Of course not."

"Then what are we doing?"

"Looking at couch options in the Hollywood Hills."

Meanwhile, I had no idea who she was. Natasha, not my friend. Or, as I now refer to her, the defendant.

The closest I ever got to any form of stalking was many years ago in New York. I was new to the city, very young, and dating a married man. Save your outrage, it was the one and only time. A girlfriend called to tell me the man I was dating was on the cover of the Post, New York's cheesiest tabloid. The picture was of my boyfriend rollerblading on a dance floor inside a club. (The 80s, when else?) My friend said a female leg was visible on the right side of the photo; she thought it was mine and called to tell me my leg was famous. The unseen image of that leg slowly drove me crazy because I knew it wasn't mine. He'd canceled that night's date with me because of a family emergency: his wife had returned unexpectedly from a trip.

Sidebar: Now that I think of it there was one more married man, so insert reader outrage here.

I obsessively combed the Upper East Side searching for a copy of the Post. In addition to devotion to your subject matter, this is the driving force behind stalking: obsession. Add neatness and an inability to exit a room without flipping the light switch less than twenty-five times and you're suddenly saddled with a three-year Klonopin prescription for your advanced case of Obsessive Compulsive Disorder.

No newsstand had the issue. They'd sold out and the afternoon version of the Post was already displayed, fanned out like a pack of playing cards on a blackjack table in Vegas, but with no picture of my boyfriend and the headless leg. I called the offices of the Post and the only remaining copies were at their distribution center. I was new to Manhattan so I wasn't familiar with their transportation system, unless you count taxis, but knowing it was a small island I figured it couldn't be that hard to locate. Two city buses, accompanied by two transfers on each, which makes two hundred and thirty-seven buses, and three subway rides to the end of the line and I emptied out in the middle of nowhere. I set off on foot, crossing fields, train tracks, dead birds. I had no idea where I was. It was mid-November and I was freezing. Eventually I spotted Canadian Mounties and an Iditarod team and knew it was time to give up and head for home.

Sidebar: This has been Suzy Soro reporting for Hyperbole News Network.

I never found a copy of that *New York Post*. Asking my boyfriend to give me one, as I was sure he'd bought all the extra copies, resulted in the lie that he had no idea what I was talking about.

And that was the sum total of my stalking. I don't even stalk my exes on Facebook. If they're doing things that don't involve getting a messy divorce or declaring bankruptcy I'm not interested.

To get all the details for this book as perfect as possible I relied on the journals and yearly agendas I've kept for most of my adult life. Even though many of the pages are tear-stained and covered in orange Cheetos dust, there were enough legible swearword-filled pages to reconstruct these stories. I also relied on the friends and family members who were with me when some of these encounters happened. If I got any of the details mixed up or wrong blame the tears and Cheetos.

Some people write books and make up names to protect the identities of their friends and family. Not me, I want everyone to know exactly who is responsible for this mess so I used real names. If a name is missing from a story that seems to warrant one and is replaced with "a friend", "an ex-boyfriend", or "the unsub", it's because they don't need any publicity from me. And I probably hate them.

And lastly, before you rush over to Amazon to leave me a hateful review, remember the illustrious words of newsman Sander Vanocur:

"A critic is someone who comes down off the mountain after the battle and shoots the wounded."

Three Point Two Five Stars

There are moments I picture myself frozen in time, a ridiculous fake smile plastered on my face, millions of people watching me on national TV, unable to do math in my head, or anywhere else frankly, and I laugh. Because that's what celebrities look like when I trap them into talking to me.

I'm a standup comic. I've played Lompoc maximum security prison, Air Force bases in California, a nudist colony, the National Cowboy Hall of Fame in Oklahoma and shows in Macedonia during the Bosnian War. I've performed in twenty-four states and eight countries. I've done thousands of shows and none of them was as nerve wracking as appearing on *Star Search*, the baby daddy of all contest shows.

When *Star Search* was on the air in the 1990s it was a big deal to be seen in front of a national television audience. Unlike today, when it appears everyone I went to high school with and the people who deliver my mail have all been on a show. Talent is no longer required, fortunately for the entire lineup on TLC and *The Amazing Race*. I'm looking at you, *Survivor*. Eating live bugs is not a talent so much as a cry for help.

I was age range 29-36. No one in Hollywood has a real age, there's only an age *range*. This implies we can play all the ages listed in that range. It's a giant lie, one we are all happy to tell. We'd play a fourteen-year-old or an octogenarian if the occasion arose, the director was blind or it paid scale. We lie about our age for a good reason. Casting directors and movie studios will automatically add five years to whatever age you say you are. So you have to deduct ten years to make Hollywood think you're only five years younger than you really are. Naturally this automatically makes us all graduates of the John Travolta School of Hiding. I remember when actor-choreographer Debbie Allen lied about her age in a *People* magazine article. Some of her jealous high school girlfriends wrote to *People* saying she used to be their age but miraculously was now younger. Relax, Chicks-Who-Never-Had-Sex-with-the-Captain-of-the-Football-Team, Debbie will regain her true age in her obituary, when she's cast in a production at Forest Lawn.

Sidebar: I made my family very aware of Hollywood ageism, so when a woman seated next to my father at a dinner party asked him how old I was he replied, "I don't know, she won't tell me."

Sidebar, Jr.: My sister Lindy once saved her neighbor's life. Based on the woman's daily activities, Lindy sensed something was very, very wrong and used her copy of the woman's key to enter her apartment, where she found her passed out. When EMS arrived, they asked Lindy a lot of questions: when she found her, how she got into the woman's apartment, how long she'd known her.

"Date of birth?"
"I'm sorry, I don't tell my age," Lindy replied.
"Not you, the woman lying on the floor."

Star Search was hosted by the avuncular Ed McMahon, perennial sidekick and foil to Johnny Carson on *The Tonight Show* from 1962 to 1992. I'd auditioned for it a few times in New York but didn't pass. The show favored the All- American Cheerleader Types; no Real Housewives of New Jersey or even old Jersey need apply. I'm not an All-American type and definitely not a *Star Search* comic. I'm not the girl next door with a bright smile and sweet little jokes. I'm sarcastic and edgy and I never smile because that's how you get wrinkles around your eyes. And my jokes? The majority are about death, dying, or the dead, or an event leading to death, dying, or the dead. My fifteen minutes of fame will probably take place at a cemetery.

The show's format was simple. One act competes against another act and then the winner of that match goes on to battle another act all the way up to a *Star Search* grand- prize winner in each of the following categories: Comedians, Actors, Dancers, Singers, and my personal favorite, Spokes Model. The Spokes Models were chosen on looks and their "talent" was doing a pretend commercial into the camera while wearing as little clothing as possible. Naturally, the comedians, actors, dancers, and singers hated them as much as they hated James Franco and Anne Hathaway hosting the 2011 Oscars.

Because of my dark persona my agent said I'd never make it on the show. (Agents only get ten percent. There's a reason for that.) But I was determined because I wanted the money. In show business you cling to the prospect of a big pay day because it's the only thing that makes up for all the heartbreak. So without warning my agent I auditioned as a happy, peppy chick. I smiled! I risked eye wrinkles! He was upset, convinced that changing my persona so radically was doing myself a disservice because in Hollywood having a clear-cut character makes you easier to cast.

When you do a contest show, performing isn't the worst part, although it's definitely nerve-wracking. The spotlights are so bright you can barely see the audience. You pray you remember the order of your jokes, all of which have been pre-approved by *Star Search*. It's the waiting for the results that's the killer. They didn't tease the audience by saying they would announce the winners...*Right after this commercial break*. That's an annoyance added by *American Idol*. So the other comic and I waited backstage, pacing. We didn't even talk to each other. I'm sure we both thought we'd won. Finally we were called to the stage by Ed McMahon. We marched to our pre-assigned marks on the floor.

"Suzy Soro, 3.25 stars. Kermit Apio, 3.75 stars."

Math? No one said there'd be math. Decimal points meant

fractions. Or was that Algebra 2? Why was my only real skill accessorizing? I stood rooted to the spot; the wheels of my brain clanking so violently against each other I was sure people at home were turning down the volume on their TV sets. You know the concentration it takes to line up those little matching tracks on a plastic baggie so they keep out all the air yet fit together perfectly? That was what my brain was doing.

Kermit hadn't moved so I thought it possible that we tied. He and I had both done well but I got two applause breaks! I had to be the winner. The audience was clapping. Was it for me? It had to be for me! I had time to get pregnant and give birth while waiting for those fractions to make sense to me.

Finally McMahon announced the winner: Kermit Apio. I like to think Kermit won because his name was funnier than mine. MY STUPID PARENTS. Thank God Ed announced a name because I would probably still be standing on that stage. A ridiculous fake smile plastered on my face, frozen in time.

I walked off stage in a humiliating daze. I didn't turn to the cameras and scream, "You'll be sorry! You've made a huge mistake you ***** idiots! I'm going to make it big!" but I probably would have if there had been cameras filming the losers. I'd like to find the moron who coined the phrase "It doesn't matter if you win or lose, it's how you play the game," because I'm pretty sure the team who loses the Super Bowl never says, "It's all good; we played well!" Ask Mitt Romney if winning doesn't matter. Or Susan Lucci.

Backstage I almost tripped over two little girls who lost in their dance category. They were sitting in a corner, crying. I told them to shove over and sat down next to them. I wanted to comfort them but it was impossible to get words out what with all the sobbing I was doing.

It does matter if you win or lose.

Amazon review by LetAvidLet: 3.25 out of 5 stars
See what I did there? I gave you the same amount of stars you got on Starsearch. Now thats funny. You probably weren't that grate on the show so thats why you lost.

Reply to LetAvidLet by JeerInScabs:
Dude, what tv shows were you on?

Me and Kermit Apio. He should have lost *Star Search* for wearing bicycle shorts under his regular shorts. I should have won because I'm not wearing any shorts.

Reply to JeerInScabs by LetAvidLet:
I found allot of money in a cab and turned it in and was interviewd on the news.

Reply by author Suzy Soro to LetAvidLet and JeerInScabs:
Before we launch LetAvidLet's reality show on Bravo can we stay on topic? And will someone please remind me what the topic is?

Twiggy, Meryl, Swoosie, Joan and a Star Search Spokes Model

In the late 70s I worked for a man we all called Hugo even though his real name was Howard. Hugo and his brother Mickey, who we all called Mickey, owned the boutique Hugo Plumm on Polk Street in San Francisco. I was one of their salesgirls, currently referred to as sales associates because somewhere along the line "girls" became extinct.

I was age range 18-26 and weighed 100 pounds due to chain smoking Marlboros in the red flip-top box and an excessive Benzedrine habit. I got more done in an hour than most people got done in a week. I had Vidal Sassoon's second-major-haircut-revolution hair, meaning short short short. I'd bleached the edges white but the crown of my head remained ash blond, my real color. From across a room I looked like a 5'6" dirty Q-tip.

Hugo and I had a brief affair while I worked for him and I always remember him fondly not because of anything sexual but because he saved my life. He and his brother used heroin but they only snorted it, which doesn't make it any less Amy Winehouse-y, but they weren't needle junkies. It wasn't long before I tried it, and if you like vomiting violently every time you get high, heroin's the drug for you. I'd done it a few times and vomited violently a few times and was on the road to John Belushi's house.

"Do you have any of that stuff?"

"What stuff?" Hugo asked.

"You know."

"No, I don't know."

"Heroin. I want some and I know you have some and I only need a little bit."

"*Need* a little bit? That's it, you're done. No more for you."

And I never did it again. It probably helped that heroin was very expensive and the dealers who sold it had tattooed teardrops under their eyes. So buying drugs from a murderer dropped quickly from my bucket list. Years later I heard Hugo had a heart attack at 29. So yeah, a little bit Amy Winehouse-y after all.

One night Hugo and I flew to Reno. I don't gamble and didn't want to go but Hugo said there would be free cocktails at the blackjack table so I figured I could stand behind his seat and steal his drinks. Because I'd never been to a casino and wasn't familiar with the dress code, I wore a clingy black one shoulder evening gown with a slit so high you could see my intestines. Once Hugo hit the tables and I stole a drink or four, I wandered off.

I walked from table to table, slot machine to slot machine and was standing by the roulette wheel when someone tapped me on the shoulder. I turned around and two girls my age range were holding pens and paper and trying not to be excited.

"Can we have your autograph?"

"Sure, who do you think I am?"

"Aren't you Twiggy?"

Twiggy? The wafer-thin English supermodel with the English accent who lived in England and was taller than me and oh yes, was English? That Twiggy?

I signed her name.

Ten minutes later another tap on my shoulder. Prepared to sign yet another fake autograph I was surprised to see a Casino security guard standing in back of me, frowning.

"You gotta leave, lady."

"Leave? Why?"

"You'll have to take your business elsewhere."

"My business? Signing fake autographs is not a business. Those girls were so excited to see me I couldn't help myself.

You'd better go away or else they'll think you're arresting Twiggy."

"Lady, I'm not going away and I'm not going to arrest you and I don't know this Twinkie person or care who you are but you gotta leave."

Not the first time I'd be mistaken for a hooker but that's another book entirely.

Years later, when I lived in New York, my friend Barry took me to see *My One and Only* on Broadway, starring his friend Tommy Tune and Twiggy! Barry and I made our way backstage after the show and when I managed to get Twiggy alone, I told her the Reno story.

"Didn't they notice you were a Yank and that you didn't have an accent and that you're shorter than me?"

"Nope, not at all."

"I'm going to try that next time, ask someone who they think I am. And if they don't guess right? I'll sign the name of whoever they think I am. Maybe I'll sign yours!"

***

When I lived in New York people said I was a dead ringer for Meryl Streep. Meanwhile, I don't look anything like her. It's easy to tell us apart if you compare our bank accounts. Or careers. Plus, I had the good sense to get a nose job.

One day at LAX, on my way back to New York, I saw Meryl approaching the terminal.

"You know, people always mistake me for you."

Was it my imagination or did Meryl look horrified? Her expression was the same as my final-result-of-Star-Search-face. Either in her head she was struggling to line up those little tracks on plastic baggies or she was trying to think of a reasonable reply. What are you supposed to say to someone who tells you you're often mistaken for them?

"Oh god NO!"
"They must be blind!"
"You're kidding, right?"

But Meryl said none of those things. Instead she smiled and said, "Sorry?"

***

I went to the American Comedy Awards at the Shrine Auditorium in downtown LA every year from 1993 to 2001. Comedians from film and television were honored along with standup comedians. Best Female and Best Male comic were chosen from a field of five and every working comedian coveted a nomination. In 1996, the year Kathleen Madigan won Best Female Comic, I was sitting at a round ten-person table in a chair that I'd turned to face the stage, which put me in the path of one of the exits.

Apparently Kathleen was tired of watching the rest of the show after she'd won.

Sidebar: The award was called a Lucy and was named after Lucille Ball but I never heard one person refer to it that way.

With her American Comedy Award in hand, she and some of her friends approached my table as they were going to exit right in front of me. I thought I'd congratulate her. I'd never met her but was a huge fan. So I was surprised when she stopped in front of me.

"Big fan, big fan, I love sisters!" she said.

Okay, I have a sister and I do love her when she's not being an asshole, but I didn't love *all* sisters.

"I watch it all the time!" she added as she and her friends walked away. It took me a minute to figure out she was talking about the TV show *Sisters*. She thought I was Swoosie Kurtz.

***

I was in a casting director's office, where everyone is automatically prettier, taller, and thinner than you, waiting to audition with a horde of other actresses. After twenty minutes an officious woman carrying a clipboard came rushing to my chair, her stilettos clicking across the floor like she was being chased by a fire.

"Oh I'm soooo sorry to have kept *you* waiting, please follow me."

I stood up and when she got a good look at me said, "Oh shit, you're not Joan Van Ark."

***

After I lost on *Star Search*, my dad, my dad's fourth wife and one of my step-nieces, all of whom were in the audience, left the theater with me. In Orlando, Florida, in the thick of Disney World, surrounded by thousands of people who hadn't recently been humiliated on national TV, my dad had a breakdown.

"I don't understand how you lost. You were so much funnier than that guy."

Dad was being a good dad. Saying all the things you're supposed to say to your child on the verge of a psychotic break. I was already embarrassed. I was the kid who always got in some kind of trouble my entire life and this felt like more of the same. How could I lose in front of my own father? Someone tapped me on the shoulder. Hoping it wasn't a security guard who was going to tell me to take my business elsewhere; I turned around to see two teenage girls.

"Did you just do *Star Search*?"
"Yep."
"Did you win or lose?"
"Lose."
"I'd like to see the Spokes Model who beat you."

So as it turned out I lost in two categories.

Amazon review by ILikedAHip: 2.0 out of 5 stars
This would have been funnier if you'd been mistaken for a man. Maybe you were and just aren't saying it. I saw your picture on the internet and you kind of look like Steven Tyler even though he has brown hair btw this is not a compliment.

Author Suzy Soro's reply to ILikedAHip:
Btw I realize that.

Amazon review by BeatARayAgain: 4.0 out of 5 stars
Are you really Twiggy? Who is Joan Van Ark is.

Author Suzy Soro's reply to BeatARayAgain:
Yes, I'm really Twiggy. Joan Van Ark is an actress who likes the word "is."

Maybe Jack in the Box Should Be My Husband

"It's a no hugging set."

That's the first thing my agent told me when I got the part on *Seinfeld*.

I was relieved because I'm not a fan of the hug. What happened to just nodding vaguely in a person's direction while muttering hateful things under your breath? I'm so anti-hug that I hunch my shoulders up around my ears and fashion my arms into shish-kabobs lashed to my torso. It's more of a shrug than a hug, a Frankenstein impersonation. This is to ward off the psychos who lurch toward you. The Mom Hugger with her snot-covered sweater and poop-stained hair who has to walk two states away for me to no longer smell her Diaper Genie. Or the Drunk Hugger who breathes on me so hard he's killed any communicable diseases I've picked up from the Mom Hugger. Or the Hugger I've Just Met: Do I appear friendly? *Look more closely.*

California is the hugging capital of the world. People hug you for the most inappropriate reasons. Mechanic finds the ping in your car? Hug. Your shrink finds the ping in your psyche? Hug. Get caught with a group of women in the middle of a 5.3 temblor during a Barney's sale? Hug Hug Hug. And steal steal steal since everyone's too shaken up to notice.

California is also the organic capitol of the world as people will tell you that everything from a zucchini to their relationship with the wind is organic, *man*. We also have a serious relationship with energy. "We're going to take photographs based on the energy in the room." That's what a photographer told my best friend, Dennison, while he was getting his headshot taken. Dennison now has the perfect mug shot should he ever end up on the FBI's Ten-Most-Wanted list.

We're the Organic Energy Hugging capitol of the world and this is why everyone hates us. If our gynecologist's office had guns we'd beat Texas as the craziest state in the Union. Although years ago a Texas girlfriend seemed surprised that I didn't know gynecologists used guns so what the hell is going on over there? You're supposed to use a speculum, for the love of God.

I've known Larry David since I did standup in New York. He and I played the original Improvisation on West 44th Street and Comedy U Grand, downtown. I've known Jerry Seinfeld the same amount of time. He and I both were regulars at Catch a Rising Star on the Upper East Side of Manhattan. Although Jerry's "regular" status was much different from mine. He could walk from his car to the front door of the club directly onto the stage. I could walk from the subway to the front door of the club directly into obscurity.

The man who booked Catch a Rising Star was not a fan of mine. But he liked my mother and rather than show his affection for her, he showed his lack of affection for me by trashing me to my face.

"I know other people think you're funny but I don't," he told me one night while we stood on the sidewalk outside the club.

"OK." I said.

"Soro," he said, "I'm sorry but I just don't think you're funny."

"I heard you the first time." I tried to walk away but he grabbed my arm.

"Soro, sooooo many comics think you're funny but I don't."

ALL RIGHT, ASSHOLE.

Months later I heard that Larry talked to him on my behalf and suggested he give me more stage time. He told him I was one of those people who says funny things but doesn't realize they can be turned into jokes. "She free-associates, so you need to put her up more."

The booker told him he didn't think I was funny. Is there anyone on planet Earth he *didn't* tell?

Larry and Jerry moved to Los Angeles to get *The Seinfeld Chronicles*, as *Seinfeld* was first titled, off the ground. I moved to LA a few years later. They were busy with their show; I was busy auditioning for sitcoms I never got and going on the road to do standup in clubs with terrible acoustics and a Radio Shack mic. We never ran into each other.

And then my agent got the call. I was going to play Barbara Benedict in an episode of *Seinfeld* called "The Dinner Party."

Sidebar: I was the woman in the bakery who got the last chocolate babka. Rabid fans call it the black-and-white cookie episode.

I didn't audition for the part. According to Larry, he called casting director Mark Hirschfeld and asked if he knew me. Mark tracked me through my agents, OmniPop.

"I don't remember you from the auditions," an extra on the set said when she found out what part I had.

"I wasn't at the auditions. Larry gave me the part."

"Who's Larry?"

Kathryn Kates, the actress who played the counterwoman in the bakery scene appeared by my side and slowly walked me to another part of the set.

"You can't tell extras that; it's a union rule that they have to hold auditions for every part."

Sidebar: That's one of the worst aspects of Hollywood. Many people are pre-cast but they hold auditions anyway. You drive across town, waste time and gas and truly believe you have a shot at a show. Then if you're lucky you get a callback with four other white women but a male Filipino wrestler with no acting background gets it because "We're going in a different direction," that direction being as far away from you as possible. Allegedly, there were four actresses who claimed to be in final callbacks for the role of Elaine. But the story that made the rounds was that when Julia Louis-Dreyfus left *Saturday Night Live* she had a holding deal in place with NBC and the role of Elaine was hers.

The guy hired to play my husband was the same guy who played the grown-up version of the bratty kid in *A League of Their Own*, a sweetheart of a guy named Mark Holton. He introduced himself and told me what part he had and I almost said, "Yeah *riiiiiiiiiight*" because Mark was not the kind of guy I would have picked to play my husband. That's another part of Hollywood I want to stab to death. In real life, if you dissect relationships, couples line up pretty evenly. Trolls with trolls, supermodels with handsome guys and strippers with Charlie Sheen. But in reel life, overweight balding guys and thin good looking guys alike get the pretty women. And if the lead male is thin, like Ray Romano, they cast his wife as bitchy, crazy or hateful, sometimes all three. Even in the Jack in the Box commercials Jack, with his giant round head, Pinocchio nose and zero hair gets the thin pretty girl.

Michael Richards was on set, along with Jason Alexander and Julia Louis-Dreyfus. And of course Jerry. I approached Michael Richards.

"I don't know whether you remember me but I met you at Phil Hartman's fortieth birthday party." He stared at me briefly and walked away, never said a word. When Richards got in trouble for hurling racial epithets at a black audience member at The Laugh Factory in 2006, I wasn't surprised. I found him hostile. Sour grapes because he snubbed me? Possibly.

By contrast, Jason Alexander is one of the nicest guys I've ever met on a set. Came right over, shot his hand out and introduced himself. I know that if I ever run into him and remind him of that episode he'll pretend to remember me and be gracious. If I ever run into Michael Richards I hope I don't.

At one point during the final shoot, I stepped on one of Julia Louis-Dreyfus's lines. The line got a laugh but I started talking while the audience was still laughing. Moments later the director yelled "cut" and I apologized to Julia.

"Sorry I stepped on your line."

"You did? I didn't notice."

"Yeah, you were getting a laugh and I started talking during it."

"Have you done any comedy before, Suzy?" Seinfeld asked.

Jerry gives good sarcasm.

I shot *Seinfeld* on Friday, January 7, 1994. Exactly ten days later I had an appointment to return to pick up the clothes I'd left behind. I hadn't even realized I'd forgotten them until I got home. It was one of those subconscious things, like when a woman leaves her hairbrush at a guy's house because she wants to see him again. Or a guy forgets his tracking device inside your vagina. I'd left my brown coat, the one I'm wearing in the episode, and a black turtle neck.

Sidebar: You wear your own clothes when you guest star on a show. The wardrobe department will add a hat or gloves and jewelry, but it's always your clothes unless you really don't have what they want, in which case they supply it. And no, you don't get to keep the jewelry, which is all kinds of wrong.

On that night of the 17th at 4:28 a.m., I couldn't sleep and got up to take a sleeping pill. As I sat back down on my bed hundreds of car alarms went off. I tried to walk to my window to see what kind of idiot carjackers were trying to steal hundreds of cars at the same time but the floor rolled lopsidedly underneath me. The roar of a thousand trains filled my ears. It was the Northridge earthquake, a 6.7, which for the uninitiated is slightly scarier than an airplane plunging to the ground and bursting into flames. I had to make it to my bedroom door because you're advised to stand under a door frame for safety. As if amidst all the piles of rubble you'll be found safely standing under a door frame magically held up by rosary beads and a four-leaf clover. Obviously I don't make the earthquake rules. Because if I did I'd add the coda: Stop sleeping in the nude, Suzy.

The earthquake lasted seventeen seconds, shorter than the time it takes to put on underarm deodorant. Felt like a year.

I found out the next day that the *Seinfeld* set was damaged by water. I pictured my clothes wearing flotation devices, swimming face down around the dressing rooms. Eventually I retrieved them but they were never the same after that. Now they want to direct.

In 1998 I had a phone conversation with LA comic Hiram Kasten, who'd heard through the grapevine that Larry David was planning a new TV show. And to prepare for it he was going to go back into standup comedy.

"You should call him," Hiram said.

"Hell no. What if he answers the phone? I'LL HAVE TO TALK TO HIM AND WHAT WILL I SAY?"

"Don't be such a baby, Soro. He put you on *Seinfeld*, you worked together in New York, call him! I have his number; it's an answering machine, you can leave a message."

So I called the number.

Larry picked up. Because if I'd wanted him to pick up he wouldn't have.

"L.D., it's Soro. I hear you're going back into standup."

"Yeah."

"So, what? You're going back into the clubs and you're not going to invite me to come see you?"

"I'm not inviting anyone. I'm doing prep for a sketch show."

"Is it going to be like the show we did in New York, where you got all the lines and I got nothing?"

Larry laughed.

He'd been the head writer on a Lifetime talk show called *Way Off Broadway* starring Joy Behar. I played one of the four rotating announcers on the show and we often did sketches with or without Joy.

"Remember what you did to me on that show? *Oh here Suzy, I want you to be in this scene and I'll ask you a question about your hair and then I'll say...* And I would interrupt you and suggest I could say you were wrong about my hair but then you'd stare at me and say, *and then I'll ask you about your outfit and say...* And I would interrupt you again and say, 'And I could answer that you must have me confused with the star of the show' and then you'd stare at me and say, a*nd then I'll say...* and to make a long story short I NEVER GOT ANY LINES IN THE GODDAMN SKETCH AT ALL."

Larry found this hilarious.

"And remember when Joy told you she didn't think one of your jokes in the opening monologue was funny? She'd asked me what I thought and I didn't think it was funny either. Then ten minutes later you showed up in her dressing room and said you needed to talk to her? And she left with you and when she came back five minutes later she sat in her chair, looked at me in the dressing room mirror and said, "The joke's back in." And then she did the joke in the monologue and it killed and got an applause break?"

"Do you remember what the joke was?" Larry asked.

"I think it had something to do with big breasts."

That was vintage Larry; all he wanted to know was which joke of his got an applause break.

"And remember when you came to my surprise birthday party which I didn't know was a surprise but you'd left a message on my answering machine before the party blowing the surprise and I heard someone whisper to you in the background that you'd blown the surprise and then you stopped talking and said, 'I have to go now', remember THAT?" Larry was roaring with laughter now.

By the time I hung up from our hour-long phone call, I was laughing too. Another person might have been insulted by my accusations but Larry knew I was right and that his behavior was funny.

I walked to the corner store while Bob Weide, the director of the special that would herald in the series *Curb Your Enthusiasm,* left me a message. I called him back and he said Larry was bumping one of the cast members and putting me in instead. I asked who Larry bumped and it was one of the male New York comics who'd been the most arrogant and mean to other comics.

What goes around really does come around, although it might take eleven years.

I'll wait.

Larry, a comic named Mike and I shot our scene in a restaurant. A waitress sets the bill down after we've 'eaten' and walks away. We shot the scene multiple times and in every take the waitress appears, sets the bill down, and walks away. And there it sat, in every take, untouched. The scene finally wrapped.

"I notice neither of you reached for the bill," Larry said.

And this is why everyone loves Larry. Even in a pretend scene where no money changes hands, because it's a *fake scene,* Larry will find a way to make you wrong.

Amazon Review by SlimLatrine: 4.0 out of 5 stars
Are you the lady who got the Marble Rye? I loved that episode.

Author Suzy Soro's reply to SlimLatrine:
The marble rye lady was a thousand years old and is now dead, so thanks for that. Based on this information it's doubtful she wrote this book. Although this is Hollywood and the miracle of rising from the dead has been proven by Betty White.

No Wonder I Never Wanted An Easy Bake Oven

I'm not in great shape. The only time anyone wrote "lots of abs" next to my name was in my attendance report from high school. So I joined a gym. You can't *not* join a gym in Los Angeles. The authorities will find out and suddenly you're on a billboard that says Got Fat?

So I Got Serious and hired a trainer, or rather hired the one that Bally's Gym assigned to me. He'd been Mr. Bulgaria twice; Mr. Northern California in the early 90s and wrote three fitness books, which was three more than I'd written. I felt sorry for him; his business card was an unevenly sliced-up piece of Xerox paper. He was earnest and committed, probably had a family waiting in a cramped one-bedroom apartment somewhere in Koreatown, expecting him to put borscht on the table. He had that sad, vacant look that people who do not ever expect to catch up with life have. I have the same expression after I've had sex.

Mr. Bulgaria loved working out and assumed I did also because why else would I be at the gym?

Sidebar: Cute guys, the smoothie bar and cute guys. Oh yes, and cute guys.

I don't understand why people love to sweat. "It gets out all the toxins." If there are toxins leaking out of any part of me it means my alcohol levels are dangerously low so point me in the direction of a martini.

Maybe I'd love working out if I enjoyed eating. Then there would be a goal, to lose weight or keep a steady weight. But I hate eating even more than I hate working out. Hand me a pill marked LUNCH and I'm done until I'm handed a pill marked DINNER. Give me a purple drink like the one in the movie *Barbarella*. Jane Fonda drinks it when she wakes up from a hundred and fifty-four hour nap. Sounds like a perfect place to live; you drink your meals and get to nap for six days in a row. That movie was made in 1963 so apparently the future has let us down. And by us I mean me.

I don't like to discuss food, shop for food or try the food at the trendy new restaurant in Who Cares, Connecticut. I lived with a man who used to drive me crazy because while we were eating breakfast he'd ask me what we should do for lunch. At lunch, he'd ask me what we should do for dinner. At dinner, he'd ask me what we should do for breakfast. No, we're not still together, why do you ask?

When I do manage to eat something I inhale the whole thing and am then surprised to discover that it *serves 4.* Four what, anorexics? I can hardly wait until I'm rich enough to have Ina Garten move in. It's the only reason I'm still breathing in and out.

The only machine I used regularly at the gym was the water fountain but I kept going because of the cute guys. And the smoothie bar. And oh yes, the cute guys. But sometime in the last few years the cute boys emigrated to marriage and the gym became a meeting place for old Chinese women. Mr. Bulgaria deftly escorts me through them as if he's afraid I'll stop and spontaneously break into a mah-jongg game.

The gym rat in our family is my sister Lindy, who once graced the cover of *Muscle & Fitness* magazine. Her nickname in college was The Body. My nickname in college was Can You Introduce Me to Your Sister. She goes around spewing communist propaganda like, "I'm really craving an apple." Please, Johnny

Appleseed didn't crave an apple. If you're at her house and want something fattening to eat, you have to lick the grease off her stove. She's always telling me I don't work out enough, that I don't do enough aerobics. Like getting up from the couch and lying back down twenty times a night isn't aerobic. Every time we have an earthquake I grab my Shake Weight so as to maximize the effects of the shifting tectonic plates. If that's not dedication to exercise then I don't know what is.

"How do I look in this bathing suit?" I once asked her.

"You look fabulous." Then ten days later she saw me in shorts and said, "You look terrific; not like you did in that bathing suit."

As for the rest of our family, we would rather die with a stent in our hearts than a deltoid on our wherever the hell the deltoid goes.

I went to Santa Monica Bodybuilding Center in Venice, California with her one day many years ago. Venice is a funky beach town best known for Muscle Beach, where men with arms bigger than my apartment parade around what looks like a playground for children, working out on machines, hitting punching bags and smiling for the tourists taking their pictures. I didn't know it but Stallone hung out at the Center and was friends with Lindy. I was having a rough time getting started in Hollywood and didn't realize my sister had mentioned it to him.

Lindy elbowed me and nearly broke a rib. Some people really should stop working out so much. I got a glimpse of her waving to Stallone, who walked towards us. I didn't even have time to ask her how I looked, which based on previous conversations probably wouldn't have gone my way in any event.

Sidebar: When I was new to Los Angeles I met Sly's brother, Frank, at a picnic. We chatted for about a half an hour and I thought, *I can date this guy. He's nice.* Then he asked me to take off my sunglasses. I did and within one minute he walked away. What*ever*, Frank.

Lindy on the cover of Muscle & Fitness Magazine

Sly Stallone is not a tall man. But what he lacks in physical height he makes up for in charm. He had that crooked half-smile going on and came towards me with his arms outstretched.

"Aaaayyy, somebody needs a hug." Obviously he never guest starred on *Seinfeld*.

Sylvester Stallone with my sister, Lindy

From the neck up my sister and I do slightly resemble each other but still, how did he know I was Lindy's sister? From the neck down we're a *Glamour* Do and Don't. Sly's bodyguards surrounded us. They were taller than Sly and me so from across a room we looked like we'd been swallowed by a redwood forest. Sly hugged me like I owed him money.

"Thank you Mr. Stallone." I said.

"Sly, people call him SLY." Lindy hissed. I wasn't going to call him Sly. How pretentious to call him Sly when I barely knew him. I'm no drooling sycophant.

"Thank you, Sly." I said.

"You know I had a rough time when I got here. Lotta rejection, lotta thoughts of quitting. Then you know, *Rocky*."

Stallone had trouble getting the movie made because he wanted to play the title role and since he was an unknown no one wanted to take a chance on him, especially since he'd also written the script.

"Aaaayyy, don't give up, it can happen to you."

After Sly and his body guards left Lindy and I began to work out in earnest. She did anyway; I was staring into space wondering if Sly noticed I hadn't plucked my eyebrows. I watched as she admired her calves. Inspected them as if they had USDA stamped on them and were going to market in a refrigerated truck. A line formed. Now other people were inspecting her calves. Suddenly one of these voyeurs took time out from his busy schedule of ogling her and eyed me suspiciously.

"What's that on the back of your arm?" he asked.

"A triceps?"

"Well," he continued, "have a doctor look at it; it might be cancer."

Amazon review by OnPlainest: 3.0 out of 5 stars
Sly and the Family Stone were not in the movie Rocky. I saw them in Golden Gate Park in 1969 and also they're African-American and I'm pretty sure Sylvester Stallone is Italian. The author has not done her research.

Author Suzy Soro's reply to OnPlainest:
And this is why some people need Adderall more than others.

Don't Call Us, We'll Call You

I didn't recognize the return address on the envelope so I tore it open quickly, leaving a jagged edge on the piece of paper underneath the flap. "Notice to vacate the premises." I read it again. Maybe this time it would say I'd won Publisher's Clearing House. The kid standing at my front door made no facial judgments but I knew he knew what was in the envelope. A lawyer paid him to deliver it so he knew.

"Didn't they get my check?"

"Dunno. Can you sign here?" He shoved a clipboard at me.

Even though you're not supposed to kill the messenger that's exactly what I wanted to do. Maybe not kill him but punch him. Definitely punch him. I took his pen and signed away my right to stay in my apartment.

When I file my taxes I'm too afraid to take two deductions. I won't leave my car parked an eighth of an inch in a red zone. I won't even put a glass up to my wall to listen to the girl next door having sex. (I'm no Banacek but she really needs to work on her fake orgasm. C+) So how did I get into this kind of trouble?

My rent was late.

Thirty-eight days late to be precise. I'd lived in my apartment for twenty years and was only forty-five cats and large, unwieldy stacks of old newspapers away from being one of the

Collier brothers. I was a cliché wannabe. And now late on the rent? Definitely closer to the Cliché Hall of Fame.

The landlords hadn't tacked on a late fee that is standard when rent is overdue. Next month's bill would have had a late fee of $50 added to it, but I didn't get next month's bill. I got this month's eviction notice. Rents in Los Angeles had skyrocketed, my neighborhood had gentrified, and the owners wanted me and my clichés out. I paid $865 a month for a one-bedroom when they were going for $1400 in the same area.

It was March of 2011 and I had five days to respond to the summons. I'd kept my landlords aware of my situation via email for the past thirty-seven days. I'd paid them two months' rent on day thirty-eight but now it was day forty-six and I needed a lawyer.

I found an agency that helped people with evictions and put their fee on a credit card. Their attorneys filed a reply for me. They did not, however, take my advice and write "Fuck You" on the document.

After I left their offices I took time out from my nervous breakdown to drive to Gelson's Market for groceries. I moped from the carbs aisle to the refined sugar aisle and prayed for a Xanax aisle. I also looked for the bleeding ulcer aisle, as the stress of losing my home had turned into gripping intestinal pain. And then I saw her, the most famous movie star in the world, Angelina Jolie. Which could only mean one thing: *I was Brad Pitt Adjacent.*

I don't normally trust brunettes in Hollywood until they've dyed their hair blonde and can't be picked out of a lineup with the rest of us, so I was reluctant and suspicious to get closer. But then again she didn't succumb to Hollywood pressure and dye her hair blonde like all the others so maybe I shouldn't be suspicious. But why was Angelina Jolie shopping in the deli section? Why do people waste their celebrity being normal? If I was a celebrity I'd buy the largest throne I could find, maybe a used one the Vatican had up on eBay, convert it into a car, and drive that sucker across country many, many times, making sure to visit every single person I'd ever met in my life. Eventually I would insist on being buried in it.

Angie was slowly inching her cart along, her son Pax straddling the front seat. A woman who I assumed was her assistant trailed next to them, checking her BlackBerry.

I immediately ran into another aisle and said to the first person I saw, ANGELINA JOLIE IS SHOPPING IN COLD CUTS AND CHEESES.

The man shrugged, "So?"

So? Why must people constantly remind me of my arrested emotional development?

I crept back up the aisle and saw Angelina hovering over a case of packaged meats. She was talking to Pax, and it appeared, from where I was eavesdropping, that he wasn't crazy about whatever she held in her hand. I couldn't hear exactly what they said because sitting in Angelina's cart with a tape recorder would surely land me on the cover of a tabloid. And not in a non-law enforcement kind of way.

She moved around a corner and I quickly followed.

I took a deep breath and stopped next to her cart. Looking directly at the sun will burn your retinas. They should extend this warning to Angelina Jolie. She's tall, 5'8". She wore knee-high black boots, a black turtleneck and black skinny jeans. No makeup except for her famous black Nike Swoosh over both eyes. I'm sure she wakes up in the morning with flawless age-defiant skin. By the time I wake up in the morning, put on all the creams and lotions it takes to regain my lost beauty, it's 6 p.m.

"I just wanted to tell you how beautiful you are."

"Thank you."

"This has been the worst day of my life and seeing you has really brightened it."

"Why is this the worst day of your life?"

"I got evicted."

AND THEN I STARTED TO CRY. Oh dear God.

Embarrassed, I walked away as fast as I could because I'm not a good crier. I never fully let loose so it looks like I'm choking and may need the Heimlich maneuver. I cursed NASA for not making teleportation a priority over going to Mars. Stupid geeks. In seconds her assistant caught up to me.

"Are you okay?" I stopped walking. But I kept crying.

"I'm going to be homeless. And my career is in the toilet. I'm in show business too."

Like adding the word "too" to that sentence would put me on the same level as Angelina Jolie. You know, *we chicks in show business.* On the brink of being homeless and all I could talk about was my career? I'm the reason people hate Hollywood. That and all the Organic Energy Hugging.

"Maybe we can help you."

I didn't know how to respond to that so I mentioned that I couldn't afford the dental work I needed. PLEASE STOP TALKING SUZY.

As Angelina's assistant scrolled in her BlackBerry, Angelina cruised by. She made a perfect U-turn around me, down one aisle, then around in back of me and up the next aisle. She never took her eyes off us. She was making sure her assistant was taking care of me. Or maybe she wanted a better look at my baggy, tear-stained sweats because she was playing a depressed homeless woman in need of dental work in her next movie.

"Give me your email address," the assistant said. "I'm sending you an email right now so you'll have ours. We're going to help you."

I mumbled thank you and walked away. I got home and there was a blank email from the assistant. This is the part of the story where I should have stopped talking about the whole thing but we all know that didn't happen.

I posted the story on Twitter. Within twelve hours I got an email from *Us Magazine.*

"Dear Suzy,
I am a reporter with Us Weekly magazine ...and I saw you tweeted about seeing Angelina Jolie... Any cute details? Did she bring the kids? How did you meet her? I'm on deadline so the sooner you get back to me the better."

Now this is really the part of the story where I should have stopped talking about the whole thing but instead I deleted all the tweets I'd made about Angelina and then sent an apology to their blank email address for getting *Us Magazine* involved. And what better way to ingratiate yourself than to write needy emails to people you don't know? *Who are famous.*

When I didn't get an immediate response I panicked and realized I might have said a thing or three about Angelina on my blog which we all know is an absolute must-read for all major movie stars. I went into the blog and rewrote any parts where I'd made jokes at her expense. There were only two, and neither was lethal, but I wasn't taking any chances of not being cast in an Angelina Jolie movie based on any snide comments I made in my blog. As it turned out I needn't have worried.

I never heard from them again. Which was weird.

Why send someone after me to check on my emotional well-being and then not contact me? Was it the email explaining the *Us Magazine* involvement? Maybe they Googled me and thought I'd try and soak them for a gig. Or money. Whatever the case I was disappointed and yet not totally surprised. After seeing hundreds of pictures of their whole family on different outings and in different countries it's obvious Angelina controls her press carefully. Paparazzi don't automatically show up on the very day you decide to take your family for ice cream in Italy. Or France, or wherever the hell they go.

Sidebar: After *The Artist* won the best picture Academy Award in 2012, the star of the movie, Jean DuJardin, was at LAX the same day Lindy and I took Mom there to head home to France. He was being trailed by paparazzi. We said hello to him in French and one of the photographers asked us who he was. We told him and he shrugged. We asked him why he was taking DuJardin's picture if he didn't even know who the guy was and he replied, "PR agent." They alert the paparazzi to appearances by their clients. It's like when firefighters do control burns to waylay an inferno.

While we're on the topic of Angelina, you can't steal someone's husband. Or anyone's husband. Or any man. Unless they want to be stolen. If you could, George Clooney and I would be living on Lake Como *together*.

As to the apartment eviction, I got the better end of the deal. My attorney got me six months of free rent and my new place is much bigger, on a higher floor, with a panorama of downtown LA, a balcony overlooking Paramount Studios, a view of the Hollywood Sign, and other things I didn't have in the old apartment. Like the will to live. In retrospect, it was the best thing that ever happened to me, as a lot of miserable things that happen to us in life often are.

If only we knew it at the time.

Amazon review by BedSoireeJunky: 5.0 out of 5 stars
I love this story because I love Angelina she is so beautiful omg the author is so lucky to have met her I hope there still in touch.

Reply to Bed SoireeJunky by JeerNMeanFat:
Did the person who gave this story 5 stars even read this chapter because if they had they'd know the author never heard from them again. The reviewer needs to learn to spell corectly and know grammar better.

I Think She Was Afraid of You

The most exclusive part of Malibu, California is called The Colony. It sits on the ocean, a gated community of really, really rich people, with its only entrance via a security guard at a gate you can't pass through without an invitation from one of the really, really rich people. You can walk onto their properties from other parts of the beach, but painfully thin women with abnormally large breast implants and Botoxed faces will stare you down if you do. They'll be angry but you won't be able to tell.

Malibu is often referred to as The 'Bu, which has two syllables, while its full name has three. Rich people don't have time to pronounce three syllables, not if they want to make a ten a.m. court time with their tennis pro, fire their housekeeper, and get a spray tan all in time to meet their lawyer and third future ex-wife in court.

To live there comfortably, it takes a large disposable income, which does not mean what it should mean: income that is thrown away. Because everyone from Shirley MacLaine and Jennifer Aniston to Britney Spears and Paris Hilton all throw their money away shopping for a $100 T-shirt, $200 lunch, or a 9 million dollar home.

Celebrities and non-celebrities live there, some permanently, others renting a house for a month or two - to write their novel, escape their difficult life in Beverly Hills, or to continue their affairs with anyone other than their spouse. The rentals start at $20,000 a month, although I hear 2012 was a difficult year and the rents were lowered to $15,000 a month. Heartbreaking.

The supermodels slouching on picnic tables while they have a hearty lunch of an Altoid and a decaf half-caff are interspersed with all the underpaid personal assistants of the rich and famous. Although it's sometimes hard to tell where Rich ends and Poor begins, finding a poor person in Malibu is as rare as finding the Winklevoss twins at Mark Zuckerberg's house. No item in any store in Malibu needs a price tag because it would just prompt the buyer to ask the sales clerk what this "funny little piece of paper" is. If INS ever shows up unexpectedly in Malibu, a lot of pissed-off white people are going to have to learn how to load their own dishwashers.

Trendy, overpriced restaurants weave haphazardly around trendy, overpriced boutiques. If it's supermodel thin, if it's trendy and overpriced, it's Cross Creek Mall, the heartbeat of Malibu. It sits off the Pacific Coast Highway with The Colony on one side and the Santa Monica Mountains on the other.

Some non-celebrities like Brian Grazer, who produced The *Da Vinci Code* and *Parenthood,* have a permanent home in Malibu.

Sidebar: Grazer was famous for divorcing his best-selling author wife Gigi Levangie right before their tenth wedding anniversary. If you make it to ten in California, it's possible to receive alimony for life. It's probably why Tom Cruise dumped Nicole Kidman right before their tenth.

I always see Grazer at Italian Restaurant Tra di Noi at Cross Creek. Grazer sits outside having lunch on the patio so he can be seen. That's how you know who isn't a celebrity or who is in Celebrity Decline: they eat outside. I eat inside at McDonald's but that's only so my fan, the guy who collects cans in my neighborhood, doesn't ask me for spare change.

A sea of black SUVs are usually parked in random groups all over Cross Creek, a few belonging to the nannies of wealthy soccer moms, and in the more remote areas, the ones belonging to the scavengers carrying cameras with zoom lenses twice the lengths of their bodies. Paparazzi. They walk around aimlessly, flicking cigarette butts into the street and waiting. Always waiting.

One day my friend Jill and I were shopping while they waited for Pamela Anderson. Jill and I wandered through the boutiques and spotted her entering the Cross Creek pet shop with her children. We ducked into the book store next door to get a better look at her once she resurfaced.

When she did, the photographers rushed her, forcing her and her kids into a run for her car.

"Pam!"

"Pam Pam Pam."

"Pam, over here!"

"Pam, do you still love Tommy Lee?"

"Paaaaaaaaaaaaaaaaaaaaaaaaaaaaaaaaaaaaam."

Even without her red bathing suit, and even though she's running at high speed and not in slow motion, her breasts straining against a skin-tight T-shirt, muscular legs in shorts so tiny I wondered why she bothered with them at all, it's easy to see why she remains a sex queen at 46.

I ran outside waving my arms like I was landing a 747 at LAX and screamed at the paparazzi to leave her alone, that she was with her kids and *to stay away from her.*

Anderson stared at me briefly, with the Did-I-Win-Star-Search-Or-Lose face as her kids clambered into the backseat of her SUV. She then jumped in the driver's seat, stared at me again, threw her car into reverse, and sped off while I was still yelling and landing that 747. After she got away and the paparazzi wandered off I went back into the book store to retrieve Jill.

"Can you imagine? She was with her kids. That was so wrong."

"You don't even like kids. You don't care what happens to them as long as they leave you alone." Jill said.

"Hey, little kids are always sticky. I don't like them touching my stuff. And besides, those guys are *assholes*. I was helping her."

"Dude, you were way worse; waving your arms and

screaming like that. She's used to the paparazzi; she was probably running away from you."

Oh.

Amazon review by ABlondeWhirl: 2.0 out of 5 stars
I saw Pam Anderson on dansing with the stares and thought this chapter would discuss that because I'm training to become a famous danser but it doesn't. Glad I got it for free out of the library.

Author Suzy Soro's reply to ABlondeWhirl:
I'm truly grateful you're not training to become a famous speller. I'm also amazed you know what a library is.

Celebrity sTalker

The Weird, The Wronged, The Divorced, and Your Name's Too Hard to Pronounce

Christina Ricci has the largest forehead to emerge since Cro-Magnons walked the Earth. It's distracting. She's an excellent actress, but in every movie she's done, from *Mermaids* to *The Addams Family* to costarring on the television show *Ally McBeal*, as a character named Liza Bump, which was Hair and Makeup code for Large Head Alert - I'm always checking her forehead for signs of alien life. Because if they staked a claim on it, and there is enough room there to land a UFO of considerable width, someone would have to tell her because I doubt she'd notice. It would be easier to see a fly on a football field.

She was standing in line at the supermarket and the man in back of me recognized her. So he said hello. She forced a brief smile, picked up a magazine from the racks, flipped it open, and covered her entire face with it. She pretended to read while the man kept talking to her. So she started answering his questions from behind the magazine, which muffled her voice. If you don't want to be recognized then don't call further attention to yourself by hiding your face behind a magazine with Kim Kardashian on the cover. Or here's a thought: bangs.

***

I've spent a great deal of time in Malibu because friends of mine own a beautiful 10,000-square-foot mansion in the Malibu hills overlooking the Pacific Ocean. Malibu is the Shangri-La of southern California, if Shangri-La had two nannies to every one child and people weighed slightly more than a candy bar. I took care of my friends' dog, an impressively sized white standard poodle named... Malibu. My friends are obsessed with Malibu, both the town and the dog.

Their home is at the top of a hill and rumor had it Nick Nolte's house could be seen from their kitchen window. I ever saw him because the only thing visible from the kitchen window was a large riding ring and a girl who rode horses. Maybe Nick was one of the horses. They seemed drunk.

I once got locked out of the massive gates that enclosed their compound, which includes a pool, tennis courts, basketball court, laundry room, sauna, massage room, and a gym. There's also an elevator. In a two-story home, because ohmygod rich people don't walk up stairs. I spent most of my time in their house using the elevator because not rich people don't walk up stairs either.

After I got locked out I punched the code into the keypad but it didn't work. After a few more tries I pressed the HELP button.

"ADT Security, this is Jack, how can I assist you?"

"I can't get the security gate to open."

"Are you the owner?"

"No."

"Owner's name?" I told him.

"Owner's phone number?" I told him.

"I'm going to call the owners now, please stand by."

"Uh, they're on a boat in Florida. And I'm outside the house here in town so good luck with that."

"Do you have the security answer to prove you're allowed to be there?"

"Maybe their housekeeper does."

"And where is she?"

"I don't know."

"Maybe she's on the boat with the owners?" Please. IF ANYONE IS GOING TO FLORIDA TO GET ON THAT BOAT IT'S ME. Fool.

"Look, Jack, I'm taking care of their dog and she's in their house, so I have to get inside."

"I can't reset the front gate without the security answer so I'm going to send a car to check things out. Will you be there?"

"Well, I *won't* be on a boat in Florida, dude."

I thought about the ADT car making its way up the dark road half a mile to where I was standing outside the gate. There are no lights in the hills of Malibu and the roads are in bad shape, full of potholes, which the owners are responsible for but never repair and where in the hell is Nick Nolte when you need him?

"How long before the car gets here?"

"Not sure, ma'am." Thanks for calling me ma'am when you can't even see me. God I hated this guy. I was ready to hang up but then remembered the owners' obsession with Malibu.

"Jack, is the security answer 'Malibu?'"

The gates swung open.

The next day my friend Jill was visiting and, since we needed coffee, we took the dog to the Starbucks at Cross Creek Mall. Malibu was a large, powerful animal, and I made Jill hold her leash while we walked to the coffee shop - Jill was younger than me and had better health insurance - in case the dog ran after a rabbit and broke her neck. If I was holding the leash and the dog ran after a rabbit and broke my neck, I'd need to be put down. Jill was a few feet ahead of me and as I came up behind her I saw she was talking to someone. Someone who was leaning down and petting the dog. Oohing and aahing.

A man standing a few feet from Jill asked me questions about the dog when he figured out Jill and I were friends. I had no idea who he was, or where he came from, he was just that garden-variety older, slightly-graying-with-a- receding-hairline rich man lounging around Cross Creek waiting to snag his next trophy wife.

Eventually I looked over at Jill and realized she was talking to Suzanne Somers and the man I'd been talking to was her husband, Alan Hamel. He already had his trophy wife. It's hard to believe I didn't spot her right away. Platinum hair, great body, tan.

Sidebar: Suzanne Somers was the first woman in the history of television to ask for the same amount of money as her male counterparts Alan Alda, from *M*A*S*H**, and Carroll O'Connor, from *All in the Family*. She asked because she, not John Ritter, who had top billing, turned out to be the breakout star of their show, *Three's Company*. She was declared a diva and fired. Welcome to Hollywood.

"Suzanne, I'm such a big fan of yours."

This is my standard opening line to celebrities. It always backfires because my mind then goes blank and I can't remember one thing about their work. The only thing I knew about Suzanne was her crusade against my best friend, refined sugar. I wasn't going to mention the Thighmaster, which will be on that poor woman's tombstone: *"Here lies Suzanne Somers. She used to be famous, got fired from a hit show, did a commercial for Thighmaster and became famous all over again."*

"You're in such great shape. You still don't eat sugar?"

"Oh God, no."

"And you don't miss it?"

"No, you get used to not having it. It's the healthiest thing you can do for your body."

"I'm addicted to sugar. Please don't kill me."

I knew that was a dumb thing to say. Why would she kill me? She didn't even know me. Once you know me of course then you'll want to kill me.

Suzanne laughed, grabbed me by the shoulders and shook me. "You *have* to get off sugar!" she said.

I'm now more addicted to sugar than ever. And have no insurance to cover my shaken shoulder syndrome.

Celebrity sTalker

***

One day on Franklin Avenue in the Hollywood Hills a car exited an Arco station and tried to wedge its way in front of my car and into three lanes of traffic going the opposite way. This is the kind of driving etiquette that Los Angelenos pick up from invading New Yorkers, and it doesn't go over well. The marauding offender was now perpendicular to me in lane two, his black Mercedes-Benz G-500 all black and boxy. The driver wore a newsboy cap and sunglasses. As he forced other cars to come to a halt, just so his majesty could ruin their day, I thought, what an asshole, he's going to kill someone.

Then I realized it was Brad Pitt and as per his standard movie contract, he can probably kill up to three people a day.

I knew Brad lived in my neighborhood. When he dated Jennifer Aniston they'd have breakfast in the local hangout, Victor's. On one day in particular, Brad and Jen were on one side of our table and Gwen Stefani and Gavin Rossdale were on the other. And I didn't talk to any of them. That alone should have qualified me for *TIME* magazine's Person of the Year.

***

I got pedicures at a little Vietnamese shop five minutes from my old apartment. One day a girl I instantly recognized from *Men in Trees*, the Anne Heche dramedy, came in. She played the part of Annie and was a great actress, very likeable. Everyone shouted, Hi Ann Marie! After she took her seat I told her how talented I thought she was. Then we struck up a fairly long conversation on acting in Hollywood. I called her Ann Marie maybe thirty-seven times.

When I got home I looked up *Men in Trees* on the Internet Movie Database. Her last name was Bergl but her first name was Emily. I thought I must have had the wrong person because that definitely was not the name of the girl I'd just talked to for an hour. I wondered why all the Vietnamese women kept calling her Ann Marie until I realized Asians can't pronounce R's.

Dear Emily,
* Don't worry that Asians can't pronounce R's; they can't pronounce Z's either. ~ Your friend, Suji*

Amazon review by OverLaidOwe: 4.0 out of 5 stars
You should have talked to Brad Pitt. Is he good looking up close? Cristine Ricci is wierd looking. I hope she doesn't read your book and sue you.

Author Suzy Soro's reply to OverLaidOwe:
I hope she does sue me. I need the publicity.

Hair Today Gone Tomorrow

"Isn't that Diana Ross?"

"I guess."

"It IS her!" I took off after her with my reluctant little sister Lindy trailing behind. I always bossed Lindy around and took the lead in all our activities. Even as a kid I was obsessed with Celebrity Talking. Lindy? Was not.

The Supremes were very big in the States. Who didn't know all the words to *Where Did Our Love Go* or *Baby Love*? But Diana wasn't with the Supremes, she was with a guy, and they were walking around the Place du Tertre doing what we were doing. Nothing.

"We LOVE you!"

"You do? Well thank you. Are you English?"

"American."

"Aren't you a little young to be walking around on your own?"

"Our Mom makes us get out of the house."

Diana Ross laughed. She obviously had kids.

Visiting our grandparents in their three-room 4th floor walkup, in the middle of a low-rent neighborhood in Paris, France, with the bathroom out on the landing was how my sister and I spent our summers. My Italian-speaking grandmother and my

Russian-speaking grandfather fought constantly in a third language, French. They also spoke Greek so the phrase "It's Greek to me" actually applied in our case. Their home was like the United Nations only here, cooler heads never prevailed. Cooler heads ate a lot of pasta and blinis. Everyone was multi-lingual in our family, except Lindy and me. My grandmother spoke six languages, my mother four, and my grandfather three. Lindy and I only spoke French and English. The shame.

The worst thing that ever happened to me up until the 5th grade was that I didn't get to be a hall patrol. I waited two years and when I finally was chosen I couldn't do it because I had to go to Paris with my mother and sister. Rehearsal time was at the end of August, when we would be in France. I was so distraught I took my teacher, Mrs. Rowland, aside and burst into tears.

"I hate my parents."

She laughed and put her arm around me.

"Suzy, this is a great opportunity for you. You'll have fun, you'll learn new things. You're very lucky."

"You don't understand. We have to go *every* year."

Mrs. Rowland removed her arm from my shoulder and put on her You Spoiled Brat face. She had obviously forgotten how incredibly painful the 5th grade can be.

The only upside of these summers was that Mom let us roam free during the day. We had no supervision, no curfews, and no rules. So we spent a lot of time at the Sacré-Coeur, the big white church on the hill, in the eighteenth arrondissement, about a mile from my grandparents. In back of the church was La Place du Tertre, an outdoor cobble-stoned square made up of cafés and portrait painters who tried to get tourists interested in buying a painting or posing for a five-by-seven black on white silhouette cut-out. I wish I still had mine. I look better in blackface and you can only see half of my head.

Lindy and I spent a lot of time among the artists, wandering around, eating hotdogs, and bothering people. And now it was all paying off because, DIANA ROSS!

"So what do you do up here?" Diana asked.

"Walk around, talk to people. Waste time."
"Do you speak French?"
"Yep."
"Well, maybe you can help me out, okay?"

Help Diana Ross? Maybe she wanted us to help her write a song! Or better yet, sing backup on a song! Yes we could help Diana Ross! We went to a café and I ordered them lunch. That was the help she needed, she didn't know how to say "grilled cheese" in French.

"I love your hair. How do you get it to curl so perfectly?" I asked her. I had stick straight hair that wouldn't curl on a bet and Lindy had curly hair that she set in beer can curlers every night so it wouldn't frizz.

"This is a wig," she said.

"It is?"

"Sure, look." And she slipped her finger under the front rim of the wig and pulled it up a little so we could see her real hair underneath. It was like discovering the Wizard of Oz was a lone man behind a curtain. Shocking and disappointing.

When I was babysitting my friend's dog Malibu, in Malibu, if I ran out of dog food I had to drive to the Cross Creek Mall pet shop to buy more. The dog didn't eat regular dog food, which I could buy across the street, at Ralph's; it had to be from the private pet shop at Cross Creek. One day I was standing at the counter, waiting for a salesperson to notice me, and I glanced outside. There was Diana Ross, flipping through a revolving rack of postcards. I left the pet shop.

"Miss Ross, I know you don't remember me but I met you once in Paris."

Diana is not the kind of celebrity you walk up to. I saw my mistake instantly in the way she looked at me. It was clear I'd crossed a boundary, which of course I had, but that was kind of my thing. I invented the whole Your Private Space Is Now My Public Space thing.

"You met me in Paris?"

"Yes, I was with my little sister and you were at La Place du Tertre in Montmartre."

"Hmmmm."

I realized this was not going well. She obviously wanted me to leave her alone. She never stopped twirling that postcard rack and scrutinizing random cards. She'd hold the card up, stare at it like she was a cashier determining whether it was or was not a fake C note, and then put it back. Her body language was Go Away. Now at this point I *should* have walked away and said something like, "Nice seeing you again," but I didn't.

"You know, the funniest thing happened when we were at that café in Paris."

Was it my imagination or did she narrow her eyes slightly?

"Hmmmm."

"I ordered your food because you didn't speak French and I did."

The block of silence that followed that statement was deafening. Was she unaware she didn't speak French?

"And I asked you about your hair…"

She stopped twirling the postcard rack and looked me squarely in the eye.

"Yes…"

And I immediately knew I couldn't now, as an adult, tell her the wig story. It was the Emperor's New Clothes and I was suddenly afraid of her. There had been stories over the years of people on movie sets only being allowed to call her Miss Ross, and leaked reports of warnings not to engage her in conversation, so maybe that's what I remembered in that instant.

"Ah, it's kind of a nothing story so I'll let you get back to your shopping."

She didn't answer me and continued spinning the postcard rack. I think you already know this encounter did not discourage me from further bothering celebrities. Unfortunately for them.

Amazon review by CRAP!BikeBidet: 3.0 out of 5 stars
I wish you'd told her about the wig story. Why didn't you ask her why she left the Supremes? It seems to me that in a lot of these celebrity encounters you never ask the questions people want to know about! I would have asked her about the Supremes.

Amazon review by TheRareLaunch: 4.0 out of 5 stars
Why were your grandparents living in France if they weren't French? I love Diana Ross but never heard of these Supremes because I wasnt alive in the 40's.

Author Suzy Soro's reply to CRAP!BikeBidet:
The next time you run into a celebrity, ask them anything you want. ANYTHING YOU WANT. Then call me from prison and tell me how it went.

Author Suzy Soro's reply to TheRareLaunch:
Oy.

If At First You Don't Succeed You Should Probably Take the Hint and Give Up

Almost a year after I launched my standup career, my sister started dating Johnny Carson. 'Launched' is probably too strong a word. 'Spit It Out Like An Olive Pit' is more like it. They met through David Niven, Jr., the son of movie star David Niven. (Obviously. Although it would be funnier if he was Spencer Tracy's son.) Johnny had a beach house in Malibu; on the ocean off Pacific Coast Highway, and David had the house next door. At the time Johnny was already dating Alexis Maas, the woman who would eventually become his fourth wife. Lindy knew about Alex but I'm not sure Alex ever knew about Lindy.

Johnny people-watched from his balcony overlooking the beach while David and his friends people-watched from theirs. Carson was always recognized and waved to anyone who yelled out his name.

That's where Johnny first saw Lindy, on the balcony next to his.

"Sweets, Johnny keeps looking over at you," our friend Janet said.

"He does?"

"Yeah sweets, you should smile at him or something."

My mother was a huge Carson fan. A French teacher with chronic insomnia and an uninteresting marriage, she spent her evenings watching Johnny and grading papers. I also had insomnia but no boy liked me and my buck teeth so I didn't even think an uninteresting marriage was in my future. I'd join Mom every night for an hour and a half, from 11:30 p.m. to 1:00 a.m., which is how long *The Tonight Show* used to be. It's amazing that I was allowed to stay up but my mother was lonely and my father never got wind of our little set-up. And he was never home when I had to take afternoon naps to catch up on the sleep I'd missed. I got some bad grades in high school and blame *The Tonight Show*. And of course my mother, who never put two and two together and realized what the problem was. For example, I've been fluent in French since I was age range 11-13 but always pulled in a D in French class. It's not like I was ever going to get lost on the Paris Metro and have to conjugate a verb to be rescued.

Sidebar: I originally spelled the word 'arrondissement' wrong in the chapter before this one. The defense rests.

So Lindy and Johnny started dating. She'd dated a lot of well-known people up until then, including Alex Trebeck (all he wants to do is stay home and cook) (when he recently had a heart attack Lindy said, "Sure, he probably used a lot of butter."), Bert Convy, (one of the funniest guys I've ever met) Alan Thicke, (all he talks about are his kids) and John Tesh (he won't stop playing the piano) but Johnny, as journalists will tell you, is what is known as a Big Get. A Big Dating Get, although Lindy didn't care about that. She liked who she liked.

Mostly she and Johnny went to dinner or spent an evening at his home but on a few occasions they went to Dyan Cannon's house. I always pressured Lindy for details on Dyan's house because she'd once been married to Cary Grant. Surely there was a picture, a knickknack or something of Cary's Lindy could steal for me. But there wasn't. And if there had been she would have kept it for herself. Selfish Selfish Selfish.

Dyan kept lots of musical instruments at her place and one of her favorite party activities involved passing them out to her guests for an impromptu concert.

Sidebar: How much do you hate Dyan Cannon right now?

Lindy played three musical instruments when she was a kid: the clarinet, the piano, and the guitar. She's left-brained, which means she knows how to read music and understand math, including fractions. She would have left that *Star Search* stage a lot faster than I did. I had trouble mastering the kazoo. 'Mastering' is probably too strong a word. 'Getting My Chewing Gum Off It' is more like it. I guess it's pretty obvious I'm right-brained.

But Lindy was terrified to play any instrument in front of both Johnny and Dyan, not to mention people she didn't know. So she pretended she didn't play any instrument at all and each time was given a tambourine. This happened twice and then the pressure of having to go through it was too stressful. After that Lindy was always 'busy' on Dyan Night.

Once, the three of them went to a big Hollywood event. Lindy was supposed to meet Johnny as he was running late, so when she spotted Dyan she was grateful not to be standing alone, looking desperate. Finally Johnny arrived and Lindy motioned for him to come over.

"Oh Lindy, no!" Dyan hissed. "You never tell Johnny to come to you, *you* go to Johnny."

My favorite Johnny story was the one about the night Lindy dressed in black leather, wore a black leather half-face mask, and drove to his house. She even rented a black bull whip and tossed it into the back seat of her Mazda RX7. And of course that was the night a cop stopped her. Apparently you're not supposed to drive your car at night wearing a mask. Lindy said the officer kept sneaking peeks in her back seat. Once she removed the mask he let her go with a warning. She refused to tell me how the rest of the night went. Thank God.

One week I went to LA to visit Lindy. 'Visit Lindy' is probably too strong a statement. 'Meet Johnny Carson' is more like it. He invited me to join them for dinner at Chasen's. We sat at a table in the middle of the room because they always sat Johnny in the middle of the room. Naturally, I was a nervous wreck but he was charming. I asked him about a female comic he often had on the show, an Australian girl named Maureen Murphy. I thought she was very funny. She was the first unknown female comic I'd seen on his show. Usually it was either Joan Rivers or Phyllis Diller. He rolled his eyes.

"Yeah, she's on a lot."

"Don't you think she's funny?"

"Yeah, she's okay. But she's on a lot because she's sleeping with Jim McCawley. (The booker) I put her on to humor him."

Sidebar: Murphy had a lot of alternative names back in the 1980s but now goes by the name Mauro Murphy, although she acts under the name Maureen. She no longer does stand-up and gave her jokes to her 98 year-old mother, who used them to audition for *America's Got Talent*.

Sidebar #2: I know a lot of useless information.

Sidebar #3: That I get off Google.

We all got pretty bombed that night. I was very 'on' as they say about comedians who can't turn 'it' off. My main goal was to make Johnny laugh. (It's a sickness.) I blame alcohol and since Johnny was a big fan of alcohol, I hoped he didn't notice how crazy I sounded. But I worried when the valet brought his car around and Lindy settled into the passenger seat. They drove off and I went back to Lindy's to say the Lord's Prayer.

A few days later Johnny invited us down to his beach house. I truly was beside myself. Like, two of me walked through his front door: Normal Suzy and Freaked Out Suzy. And once again, I was 'on'. Like a smoke alarm signaling a fire, I wouldn't turn off. But Carson laughed at everything I said because I was knocking myself out at this point. If my head flew off and spewed blood everywhere, but Johnny laughed at that? *Don't take me to an E.R.*

He showed me his house, played his drums (not a euphemism), and after an afternoon of watching people on the beach and listening to all my highly inappropriate comments, Johnny wrote something on a piece of paper and said, "Call this number and tell Jim McCawley that I want you to be seen for the show."

I'd been doing stand-up for eight months. Stand-up takes many, many years to get five clean and appropriate TV minutes, and I had about thirty-two seconds of television-ready material. Maybe less. I knew I would never make the cut.

Sidebar: Right person, wrong time; timing really is everything. Ask any comedian.

I never called McCawley. I didn't want to embarrass myself and make Johnny look like he'd made the wrong choice. Everyone knew Carson never made a wrong choice over a comedian.

I moved to LA in the 90s. By then I'd been doing stand-up for eight years. My agent got me an audition for the same *Tonight Show* booker Johnny mentioned, Jim McCawley. I decided not to tell him about my previous relationship with Johnny. When you do stand-up, you obsess over the guy in the third row with the crossed arms and a scowl on his face. The entire room can give you a standing O but if Scowly McThirdrow doesn't, it will haunt you for days. What would I do if I didn't get the show after telling McCawley I knew Johnny, and that he'd offered to help me all those years ago? I would be haunted for life.

I was auditioning along with two male stand-ups from my agency. The night went well and we all had terrific sets. My agent was confident.

"Of all the comics I've seen audition for *The Tonight Show* over the years, you're the only one I saw Jim McCawley applaud." I thought the gig was a lock.

Days went by. I heard nothing. Finally I called my agent and asked him what was going on and he said that *The Tonight*

Show had picked one of the two guys from our agency. I asked him if they'd said anything about me and he said no. I asked him if he at least mentioned me to McCawley and he said no. When I asked him why he said, "I didn't want to rock the boat."

I hear those words in the middle of my nightmares where I'm naked in front of strangers and running down an unfamiliar street trying to get to the math test I never studied for.

Soon after I lost on *Star Search*, comedian Phil Hartman asked his friend, Dennis Miller, to watch a set of mine to see if I was right for Dennis's brand new talk show. I paced waiting to go on at The Improv on Melrose and Jimmy Brogan, the new, mild-mannered booker for *The Tonight Show,* now starring Jay Leno, asked me why.

"You know I got *Star Search*?"

"YOU got *Star Search*??" He was so shocked I think he thought I said I'd killed a man.

"Phil Hartman brought Dennis to see me for Dennis's show."

Dennis was one of the most well-respected comics in the business and Phil Hartman was one of the funniest guys in the business. At this point *The Tonight Show* had been considering me every now and again for a few years, and I couldn't wait any longer for my agent to "not rock the boat."

Even though The Tonight Show always thought I was too 'edgy', which meant my jokes were not safe for their audiences, I told myself Jimmy had to be rethinking the many times I'd been rejected yet now had Phil Hartman and Dennis Miller looking me over.

Sidebar: This edginess also applies to actors and actresses. All guests on any talk show are given pre-screened questions, except maybe for *The Jerry Springer Show.* Talk shows prefer guests who aren't unpredictable, like scary actor Crispin Glover, star of the movie *Willard*, who started karate kicking thin air on David Letterman's show back in 2003. Letterman was so freaked out they cut to commercial and Glover was gone when they returned.

"I changed my persona so I could get *Star Search,*" I said.

"You shouldn't have done that; you're good at what you do." Jimmy replied.

"So, are you ever going to give me the show?"

"Uh, no." Brogan said. I guess I wasn't quite good enough at what I did. After that, the boat would cease to rock for all time.

All comedians who worked during the reign of Johnny Carson will tell you their biggest regret was not getting on his show. Johnny retired from show business in 1992.

On Lindy's birthday, May 22.

Amazon review by AsInNowDear: 2.0 out of 5 stars
If you didn't get chosen to do the tonight show it's because your not funny. I think Jay Leno is the funniest comedian on tv and so is Larry the cable guy.

Author Suzy Soro's reply to AsInNowDear:
Yes indeed, Larry the cable guy, a comedy genius. Ditto weatherman Al Roker.

Amazon review by InCrankyAm: 4.0 out of 5 stars
I miss Johnny. Jay isn't funny and never puts on funny comedians because he's afraid they'll be funnier than him.

Author Suzy Soro's reply to InCrankyAm:
Is that the reason you're cranky?

The Queen of Nice and the King of Not Nice

In 1984, when Rosie O'Donnell was 22 years-old, she won *Star Search* and took home the top prize of $100,000. In 1984, I was age range 21-27 and waiting on tables in New York City, where I took home the top prize of fallen arches.

Rosie was at the top of the stand-up heap while I was at the bottom, praying for a 2:00 a.m. Tuesday night slot at the Improvisation on 44th Street, which paid $8.

The stories about Rosie's early days in stand-up are well documented. She stayed in comedy condos before she turned 21. Male comics brought their girlfriends with them and she could hear them having sex in the next room. One guy brought a gun. Eventually she found the lifestyle, not to mention the filthy condos, so degrading she refused to stay in them. She asked to be put up in hotels and if bookers didn't comply, she wouldn't work for them. I always admired her for that as I'd stay in a parked car in a Portland airport to get stage time at a bowling alley two states over. (What better place to tell jokes than to a room full of people playing with giant, thundering balls?) Rosie knew how to stand up for herself; she wasn't afraid to say No and never compromised her self-respect.

I played the 'Stop at the Trop' at the Tropicana Hotel in Atlantic City and owner Bob Kephart had a large three-bedroom condo available for the comics, much grander than any comedy condo I'd ever seen. And cleaner.

"I wish Rosie would play here," he told me one night after a show.

"She doesn't stay in condos so she probably wouldn't come."

"You know her? Have her call me if you see her. Maybe we can work something out."

I saw Rosie a few weeks later at Catch a Rising Star in New York. We weren't friends but in stand-up, you know everyone even if you don't "know them."

"Kephart wants you to play the Trop."

"You told him I don't stay in condos?"

"Yeah, I told him." She didn't have a big reaction and I assumed that was the end of that.

It wasn't. She called Bob and he put her up in a hotel room at The Tropicana. He might have put us all up but we hadn't asked. And we hadn't won *Star Search*. Especially me.

In 1991 Rosie hosted a program on VH-I called *Stand-up Spotlight* that filmed in Pasadena. I'd just arrived from New York and now don't remember how I got the show because I'm age range Has Anyone Seen My Keys?-One Foot in the Grave. It might have been from my new LA agents or via an asshole manager I had back in New York.

Sidebar: All his clients had to pay him $50 a month for all the "paperwork" and "Xeroxing" he allegedly did. He must have been copying the Library of Congress because there was that much Xeroxing according to him. So between the $8 spots at the Improv, $20 spots at Comedy U Grand, $10 spots at Catch a Rising Star and the $50 paid to my manager, I began each month $12 in the hole.

Sidebar, Jr.: Dear Mom and Dad, I told you it was a waste of money to send me to college. THIS IS WHY.

Before the taping, Rosie took all the performers aside for a discussion about what she expected from us.

"No man bashing, no woman bashing, no gay bashing, no black bashing, no ethnic bashing, no bashing *at all*."

Apparently this admonition went in one ear and out the other because I did this joke on the show: *I don't think people should break up, I think the man should just die.* Suddenly the men in the audience started to boo me. Then the women in the audience started booing the men. And everything ground to a halt. I had to wait until the booing subsided before I continued. The time it took for that to happen made my run-in with understanding fractions on *Star Search* seem like a split second. I'd never been booed before. Audiences can heckle but it's rare that they boo. You have to say something really hateful for an audience to go that far. Think Michael Richards bombing at The Laugh Factory.

I'm a comedian and *my job* is to make people laugh. If a joke gets a laugh, I keep it, if a joke doesn't, I throw it out. That joke about men always got a laugh. No comedian, at least no good comedian, no *funny* comedian, is politically correct. And political correctness had not yet, in 1991, swept the country and ruined everyday conversation, not to mention newspapers and the Internet, where people wait behind screen-name bushes with their moral superiority, dying to trap some hapless individual who uses words they don't approve of. Back then the only moral superiority came from the networks in charge of shows. And Rosie O'Donnell. In fairness to Rosie, even though we all knew she was gay, the rest of the world didn't. She obviously had a higher personal stake in any kind of bashing.

Days later I got a handwritten note:
"Dear Suzy,
Thanks so much for being a part of Stand-up Spotlight. All the best for future success. Best, Rosie."

Maybe she hadn't noticed my set. Maybe she was in the restroom when I was on stage. When I got my VHS copy of the finished show, my Boo Fest had been cut, including the joke that launched it. So, she noticed.

Very Long Sidebar: The next time jokes of mine went AWOL was when I watched the edited tape of my *Star Search* show. They'd edited out this one: *I've never been married but I have had a similar experience. I was once hit by a car and left by the side of the road for dead.* It was one of two jokes that got an applause break. I couldn't figure out why they would cut them. At first I thought it was all because of Mr. X, a manager who booked The Comedy Zone in Orlando. If you got *Star Search*, you also got a week performing at that club. When I arrived I was surprised to see that I was the emcee, not the middle act, which was my usual position in the line-up. As the emcee I had to warm up the crowd, practice as many jokes from my upcoming *Star Search* set as I could, and pull business cards from a fish bowl to give away a prize, *a pair of flip flops*. Nothing says comedy like free flip-flops. I told Mr. X that it was going to be difficult to work on my *Star Search* set but he said that was the only position he could give me. The middle act, who was not doing *Star Search*, could easily have emceed. But no. It was a huge insult. Welcome to Women In Stand-up Comedy circa the 1980s.

Still The Very Long Sidebar: The audience that week was rough. They hated me and they hated the middle act. By the time the headliner came on, they were exhausted from all their hating so they gave him a warmer reception. One night I cracked and started saying 'Fuck Me' after each joke that bombed. And the audience laughed. The middle act picked up that swearing was the ticket to them not killing us, so he started swearing too.

"I hear you've been swearing a lot," Mr. X said over the phone, the third night of the week.

"I wouldn't say it was a LOT."

"I'm getting complaints."

"From who?"

"Audience members."

I knew he was lying. Unless you've said something really hateful to them personally, they don't complain.

"What did they say?"

"Look Suzy, just stick to your little *Star Search* jokes, ok?"

My *little* Star Search jokes. What an asshole.

That night I mentioned to the other two guys on the show that I'd been reprimanded and the middle act said he had been too. So he and I went back to not swearing which meant we went back to being hated by the audience.

Stop The Sidebar I Want To Get Off: When I got to the *Star Search* rehearsal, Gary Mann, who helped produce the show, took me aside.

"This week we have no female judges. We always have at least two. Two men, two women. We try to make it as fair as possible for both the men and the women in all the categories to avoid bias, but not this week. It's all male judges."

I didn't think this would be a problem. I thought my act could sail by four male judges, and was confident my jokes were funny enough to circumvent any bias because... I'm an idiot.

"And one of the male judges is Mr. X, who I heard you had a little problem with at the club."

"Yeah, that's a big problem for me, having him as a judge. He got mad at me for swearing."

Dave, another producer, joined the conversation.

"I'm going to have a talk with him, make sure he knows not to show prejudice against you because of what happened."

After this "talk" Dave assured me Mr. X wouldn't have a problem being fair. But the one thing you learn early in stand-up is that men in power don't like being criticized.

Sidebar From Hell Just Gets Longer and Longer: Mr. X was Las Vegas comedian Carrot Top's first manager, having spotted his enormous earning potential before anyone else. In exchange for managing him, Mr. X took fifty-percent of Carrot Top's total earnings and locked him into a five-year contract. So maybe he did have a problem being fair.

Very Long Sidebar Continued And If You Hate This Chapter

You're Probably Not The Only One: Sitting in my apartment in the Hollywood Hills watching the original airing of my *Star Search* episode, I felt something was off but didn't know what. It wasn't until I watched the edited tape weeks later that I realized the edits made my set shorter than Kermet Apio's, the winner of our match. There was more of him to watch. I think that's the only way they could justify him winning because I WAS FUNNIER and the audience at home would have seen that. I'm guessing the producers saw it too and called for the edits. Years later I ran into Mr. X at the Comedy Awards. I smiled and decided to be the bigger person, but he quickly turned away from me. If I wasn't clear that he'd made sure I didn't win my *Star Search* set that clinched it for me. He was afraid to talk to me. Because he knew that I knew.

> So, sorry Rosie.
> And fuck you, *Star Search*.
> Double fuck you, Mr. X.

Amazon review by TVByLeyte: 3.0 out of 5 stars
The author has sour grapes because she didn't win a stupid show back in teh 1990's. and those sidebars, I think she means sidecars. How long are you going to keep talking about losing that stupid show???

Author Suzy Soro's reply to TVByLeyte:
Until I win.

The Perfect Mom

The first time I met June Lockhart was the day June picked Lindy and me up and we accompanied her and her friend Paul to a production of *Phantom of the Opera*. Even though I hate musicals. I refuse to suspend disbelief long enough to believe that two people walking down a street and suddenly accosted by three strangers from stage right is grounds for all five of them to spontaneously break into song. Unless the song is called "This Is Really Ridiculous and Totally Unbelievable."

Sidebar: Lindy is June's personal trainer. June Lockhart, 87, works out. Suzy Soro, age range Who Is Tired Of This Joke Already-1000, does not.

"You know June; I loved *Lassie* when I was a kid."
"I'm very proud of that show."
"And I loved that kid who played your son, Jeff?"
"You mean Timmy," June said.
"I thought his name was Tommy."
"Tommy was the actor who played Jeff."
"Oh. Well, I loved the whole Miller family."
"You mean the Martin family."
"Oh. Well I especially loved you as the mother, Ellen Martin."

"You mean Ruth Martin."

"Did you even watch the show, like *EVER*?" Lindy asked. There are days I don't think I'll let her make it to her next birthday. I decided to keep my mouth shut for the rest of the ride to the theater. Maybe June would forget I was there. I leaned into my evil sister and mumbled, "Do you believe we're in the car with Lassie's Mom?"

"You know Lassie had a canine Mom, right?"

"Shut up; stop trying to ruin it for me. Should I ask her what happened to Lassie?"

"She's probably going to say 'Dead.'"

"STOP TRYING TO RUIN IT FOR ME. You know Lassie's Mom never punished Jeff or Timmy or whatever that kid's name was? She never got mad at him. Not once. Not like our Mom."

"You were the only one who got punished in our family and Mom only got mad at you."

"I wish Lassie's Mom would have been our Mom."

"Mom probably wishes Lassie's Mom had been your Mom too."

I pictured the differences between my Mom and Lassie's Mom:

My Mom: Do your homework.

Lassie's Mom: Timmy, lie down and take a nap while I do your homework.

My Mom: Do your chores.

Lassie's Mom: Timmy, you spent all day in school, I'll do your chores.

My Mom: Stop walking around in a daze. One day you're going to fall down a well on a forty-five acre property owned by a kindly rancher in the middle of nowhere and you'll never be found.

Lassie's Mom: Timmy, we got you a dog that can find you if you fall down a well on a forty-five acre property owned by a kindly rancher in the middle of nowhere.

June Lockhart and Lindy (2011)

June Lockhart and two of her family members have three stars on the Hollywood Walk of Fame. And if you're not impressed by that statistic maybe you'll be impressed by this one: my family has walked on the Hollywood Walk of Fame. June's last TV series ended in 1968, yet her autographed headshot sells for $100 at Sci-Fi conventions.

As Ruth Martin, Lassie's Mom, and Maureen Robinson, the Mom in *Lost in Space*, June remains an icon of kinder, gentler television. *Lost in Space* inspired so many future astronauts that NASA uses June, and Nichelle Williams, Uruhru from *Star Trek*, for recruitment purposes. She's so well known in the aerospace industry that when she flew to Chicago recently, the entire flight crew stopped by her seat to say hello. When Endeavour arrived in Los Angeles in September of 2012, for its final resting place at the

California Science Center, June was at the welcoming ceremony. She was once allowed in Mission Control so she could talk to the astronauts as they orbited.

June Lockhart and Lassie

Sidebar: I'm intimidated by June. She's one of the most confident people I've ever met but she's also very bossy. At my mother's surprise birthday party in 2011, someone kept turning the music down. Then I would have to turn it back up. Then someone would turn it down again. Guests kept complaining that the music was too low. Eventually June came to me and admitted that she was the one turning the music down. I'm not shy. I also don't have a problem telling people off, but in June's case I smiled and nodded and headed immediately for the bar.

June, Paul, Lindy, and I continued driving to the theater. We kept encountering construction sites, blocking our every move. If she turned left there was a dead-end, and if she managed to turn right she'd eventually find a detour that led us in the opposite direction from where we wanted to go. We traveled up and down the same streets over and over as June got more and more agitated. She made one final turn onto a street that looked promising only to deposit us in front of the largest collection of John Deere vehicles and equipment outside of their factory in East Moline, Illinois.

"FUCK!" June yelled.

It might have been my imagination but I'm pretty sure those construction sites smiled and nodded and headed immediately for a bar.

Amazon Review by PigLikeCRACKHITMAN: 4.0 out of 5 stars
I loved Lassie and Lost in Space growing up. I wish the author had told us what happened to Lassie. I'm curious!

Author Suzy Soro's reply to PigLikeCRACKHITMAN:
According to June, Lassie is living on a forty-five acre property owned by a kindly rancher in the middle of nowhere.

Comedy Gold

One of the first jobs I got in New York was as a stand-in for Betty White on the sitcom *Love, Sidney*, starring Tony Randall. It was the first television show about an openly gay man and also starred Swoosie Kurtz, one of the stars of *Sisters*, who comedian Kathleen Madigan would confuse me with at the American Comedy Awards twenty years later.

Betty was a guest star that week and even though there's a considerable age difference between us, stand-ins are all about height, weight and hair color, not age, unless someone's been lying to me all these years. Stand-ins are used to configure lighting cues for each of the scenes as well as block the movement of the actors for the director, who in this case was Tony Mordente.

Sidebar: Tony would go on to direct TV shows like *7th Heaven*, *Matlock* and *Jake and the Fatman*. In 1987 you could use the word Fatman in a title; try doing that today and about two million people would have a cow. A very fat cow. Even though the actor who played Jake, William Conrad, was indeed fat.

I was a fan of Betty White from her days on *Password* with her late husband Alan Ludden. She had perfect timing and was sarcastic in the most ladylike way. And I knew that she and Alan had been madly in love. I was dying to talk to her but generally stand-ins are on set while the people they represent sit on the sidelines. But once Mordente called a break, I dashed over to her and stuck my hand out.

"Miss White? I'm your stand-in."

"Oh honey," Betty said, looking me up and down and laughing, "you have a terrible agent."

I got my first, and last, stand-in kiss doing that show. The script called for Betty to kiss Tony Randall. While Tony's stand-in and I were blocking the scene, Mordente yelled "Now kiss!" They never give stand-ins the script so we were both probably thinking the same thing - "You mean each other?" Another awkward moment passed and then we leaned in for a kiss so chaste it was like kissing the Pope. Not that I know what that's like but I'm going with pasty, passionless, and parental. It was as believable as the pretend kiss between Phoebe and Chandler on that episode of *Friends* when Phoebe and Rachel are trying to trap Monica and Chandler into admitting they're a couple.

On the next break I told Betty I'd watched her and her husband, Alan Ludden, the host of *Password,* as a kid. Old people *love* it when you tell them you were in-utero when you first saw them. I said I envied her long marriage to him and was sorry that he died in 1981. Her eyes lit up and she sighed. The kind of sigh that signaled a memory remembered as perfect and reminded me that I've never sighed like that.

"Yes, he was a very special man. I was very lucky."

"I'm sure you'll meet someone else one day."

"Oh, no. I could never find someone as wonderful as Alan. I had my Prince Charming."

***

The first time I met another Golden Girl, Bea Arthur, was at her home in Brentwood, west of LA, near O.J. Simpson's now-demolished house on North Rockingham.

Bea's part of town doesn't look like the Los Angeles seen in television or movies. For starters, some residents keep their horses in their front yards whereas most of us keep ours in our imaginations. Her street looks like Montana or some other rugged part of the West where you can't get a pedicure but can get a Cactus Sandwich.

Bea and Dennison, my best friend, met doing a production of *Afterplay*, which ran in Los Angeles for eight months. They'd remained friends after it closed and he'd get invited to her family dinners every now and then. After those dinners I'd pepper him with questions. Is she funny in real life? What's her house like? Have you ever tried on a pair of her shoes while she wasn't looking?

One day Bea was feeling under the weather and Dennison asked if I wanted to come along while he brought her chicken soup. We arrived about 4 p.m. and entered through her kitchen. We hadn't been there five minutes when she asked us if we wanted a drink. I was star struck and also kind of scared of her. She was a tall, physically imposing woman; a woman you could tell took no shit from anyone. I was afraid if I asked for water, the standard health-conscious answer in Los Angeles, she'd think I was a health nut, a person who would insist on vegan water, which doesn't exist, but in case it does I'm moving to Montana and giving up pedicures.

"Do you have any vodka?"

That was cheating as I'd learned from Dennison it was her drink of choice. Bea drank straight vodka from about 4 to 9 p.m. and then went to bed. Then she would wake up around midnight and watch TV. At parties at her house, dinners were early because she tossed guests out at 9 p.m. But when she performed? Didn't drink at all.

I was dying to see her house but she offered no tour, no "Make yourself at home." So the only thing I remember was that we sat at her rectangular wooden table in the kitchen and she and I drank vodka while Dennison drank wine.

Bea had two Doberman Pinchers. A Dobie with cut ears is one of the most beautiful but scariest looking dogs in the world. Bea was an animal lover so she didn't have their ears cut, which made them look like big old friendly puppies. I forgot how snappy those dogs can be and played a little too roughly with one of them and he bared his teeth and took a swipe at my arm. I didn't think Bea noticed but when I stole a look in her direction she'd fixed me with a death-lock stare.

Paul Dooley, Bea Arthur, Marian Mercer, Dennison Samaroo in Afterplay at the Pasadena Playhouse

As we drank, I asked Bea about her career. We talked about why her shows weren't, at that time, in rotation on TV Land, but were on in Canada. I'd been on tour there and seen reruns of *Maude* and that's why I brought it up.

Sidebar: Bea played Edith Bunker's liberal feminist cousin on *All in the Family* in 1971. A studio executive noticed her and said "Who's the new girl? Let's give her her own show." Bea Arthur, the new girl, was 50 years-old at the time. She'd appeared exactly twice on *All in the Family*, and Norman Lear was ready to hang an entire show on her. Today a new girl the studios are interested in is about fourteen and they'll audition half of Hollywood to find her. But substitute a male Filipino wrestler with no acting background at the last minute because "We're going in a different direction."

After *Maude*, I brought up *The Golden Girls* and told her it was one of my Dad's favorite programs. I asked Bea whether she missed doing the show and of course inquired after Rue McClanahan, Estelle Getty and finally, Betty White.

"I couldn't stand her."

"Who, Betty? Why? I mean, she seems so harmless."

"Because," she said in that throaty drawl of hers, "she was a cunt."

I remembered hearing a story years and years ago about how 'someone' used to take dumps in Betty's trailer's bathroom and never flush. It was often rumored to be Bea. Fictional or not, after that day at her house I thought it might be true.

The last time I saw her was at her one-person show here in Los Angeles, "Bea Arthur - Just Between Friends." Dennison had dragged me out of the house during a particularly bad Boy Broke My Heart depression and forced me to go. Bea was in her early 80s by then and preparing to take the show to Broadway, where it was eventually nominated for a Tony award. Because she was an excellent cook, she opened the show with a recipe, and Bea intoning any variation of 'Add sugar and stir' was invariably funny. When I'm in my early 80s I'll be preparing to take my show to a crematorium where the only recipe will involve me and a bunch of chemicals.

Dennison and I went backstage to congratulate her. She was humble and charming and always, always funny.

Bea Arthur's last appearance on TV was in 2005, on *Curb Your Enthusiasm*. In a case of inspired casting, she played Larry David's mother.

Amazon Review by WornDismay: 2.0 out of 5 stars
If this is what passes for humor these days then America is doomed! This is an example of Writing One Oh None! I miss Bea Arthur! The only thing good about this book is there's no mention of the Kardashians!

Author reply to WornDismay:
Joke's on you. I mentioned them.

White People Can't Clap on the Beat

When Lindy relocated to New York from Paris, she moved into my apartment on the Upper East Side. I was age range 22-29 and she was age range three years younger, although over the years and through the magic of lying, I now refer to her as my older sister.

She arrived with a portfolio of photos and immediately got an agent, modeling jobs, and commercials. When you grow up with a sister who is considered The Pretty One, you'd better figure out how to get attention in another way unless you like being stampeded by boys trying to get to her. Although my mother says I was funny when I was eight years-old, I'm sure I got funny when Lindy turned five and had a 34C cup.

Female Sidebar: Lindy was chosen as the original Jordache Jeans girl. Jordache was the first jean company to launch models wearing jeans for TV and print. She turned down the job because it wasn't a union gig. The girl they eventually chose went on to get a PhD while Lindy moved to Los Angeles and went on to an aerobics phase better forgotten. Lindy will not wear Jordache jeans to this day.

Lindy met Ford model Jack Scalia on one of her auditions.

**Lindy was 13 years-old in this picture.
Boys never had a chance**

Male Sidebar: Jack was the man chosen to represent Jordache Jeans. He was recently arrested at LAX for carrying a gun and at first I thought it was a publicity stunt. But he's not filming anything, so I guess not. Nice try, though.

Lindy and Jack started dating and after I met him a few times, I was instantly envious. There's Hot and then there's HOT, and Jack was definitely the one in caps.

One day he returned to New York after a location shoot and they agreed to meet at a midtown restaurant for dinner. When she arrived, he wasn't there. But composer Burt Bacharach was. Burt got her attention and said, "Waiting for someone?" She nodded and he replied, "Me too." As the minutes ticked by, Burt gave her his phone number and said to call him. Although both of their dates eventually showed, Lindy knew Jack was on his way out and Burt was on his way in. She called him.

Lindy fell madly in love with Burt Bacharach. He was bi-coastal then, living both on East 57th Street in New York and in Los Angeles. He was separated from actress Angie Dickinson but since they shared a daughter, he talked to her often.

I was dating a plastic surgeon that, like me, was a big fan of Burt's music. So when Lindy invited us to Burt's for drinks, we went. Burt was an incredibly handsome man, tall, with slightly graying silver on a helmet of coal black hair. Blue eyes. His hi-rise on East 57th was mid- century modern with a black baby grand piano in the living room. It overlooked a view of Manhattan that I never saw because when you're age range 22-29 the only view you're interested in is your own, in a mirror. The biggest surprise of the night was Michael McDonald, the lead singer of the Doobie Brothers, who was sitting in the living room as if that was completely normal.

It's not hard to be impressed with Bacharach. With lyricist Hal David he created some of the most memorable songs in pop history, a lot of them sung by Dionne Warwick.

My boyfriend pulled out a joint, lit it, and passed it to Burt. The idiot plastic surgeon was going to get us all arrested. But then I realized we were with *musicians*. If they don't smoke pot then they might be narcs. Burt brought out a bottle of champagne and between the weed and the champagne, we all got pretty high. So high that I could only think about sitting in the living room of the man who wrote my all time favorite Dionne Warwick song, *Walk on By*. I asked Burt to play it.

"Nah, I don't play that anymore."

The room got quiet. And that, boys and girls, is why you should never do drugs, because the odds of you embarrassing yourself are higher than Bob Marley ever was.

"Oh come on Burt, play the song." I had a surprising ally in Michael McDonald.

"No," Burt insisted.

I'd always had a crush on McDonald. Not only did he have a gorgeous voice but he was laid-back sexy. And now he was trying to get Burt Bacharach to sing me my favorite Dionne Warwick song. I was definitely going to marry him as soon as I drugged him, tied him up with rope and kidnapped him. McDonald wouldn't let it go. Whether he wanted to show off his singing, which was better than Burt's, or he felt sorry for me sitting there rejected and dopey looking, he went to the piano and sang *Walk on By*. Now where was I going to get chloroform at this late hour? It was so beautiful until my boyfriend attempted to clap and white people can't clap on the beat, especially when it's a slow song. And who the hell claps to a slow song unless they're smoking pot?

Another one of Burt's friends and collaborators was Paul Anka. Anka is famous for lots of 60s pop music like *Diana* and *Put Your Head on My Shoulder*. He also wrote Tom Jones's big hit, *She's a Lady,* and the lyrics for Sinatra's *My Way* as well as the theme song for *The Tonight Show* with Johnny Carson.

Months after the night at Burt's house, my phone rang at 3:00 a.m. That phone call changed my life forever because after that, I never had a phone in my bedroom again. If someone needed to call and tell me somebody died, I was pretty sure they'd still be dead in the morning.

"Suzy?"
"Ummm... yeah?"
"It's Burt."
"Oh, hi."

I said Hi but I had no idea who this 'Burt' was.

"Paul's on the line from Vegas."
"OK."

I said OK but I had no idea who this 'Paul' was.

"Suzy?"
"Ummm, yeah?"
"It's Paul. Paul Anka."

Ohhhhhh, THAT Burt. And Paul Anka?

"We're writing a song and Lindy said you were great at titling things."

It was one of my many useless gifts that don't pay, like correctly guessing the name of the celebrity doing a voiceover as one of Frasier Crane's patients on his radio show.

"She gave me your number. It isn't too late to call, is it?" Burt asked.

"3:00 a.m.? Who the hell isn't up at this hour in New York?"

Me for starters.

AND THEN PAUL SANG ME THEIR SONG. I gave them three or four titles but have no idea whether they used any of them. Burt and Lindy broke up soon afterwards. I hoped it wasn't because of my title attempts.

Years later, after I moved to LA, Lindy and I ran into Burt and his current wife, Jane, at The Ivy at the Shore, a restaurant in Santa Monica. We stopped by his table to say Hi and not only did Burt remember my name, but he also asked me how my career was going.

He never mentioned the song.

Amazon Review by RelaxAndAsOrAs: 2.0 out of 5 stars
Obviously you don't have kids because if you did then it's very irresponsible not to have a phone by your bed.

Author Suzy Soro's reply to RelaxAndAsOrAs:
I might have kids. I'll have to look around since I haven't cleaned for a while.

The Rock Star, the Movie Star, the Governater, and You Look Hotter in Person

Lindy gave the Rolling Stones cocaine. This straight A student who never gave my parents an ounce of trouble was buying them coke. They'd give her French francs; she'd score and return with their change. That's right, Miss Goody Two-Shoes may have been doing something illegal but she wasn't about to be branded dishonest. Lindy and I were both living in Paris with our Mom, because we were not entirely stupid. Go where the best food is - France. Go live with the parent most likely to pay your bills – Mom. Lindy was dating the Stones' guitarist, Ron Wood, and I was starring in a French cabaret show at *La Nouvelle Eve*, a music hall in Pigalle.

Sidebar: I was the second American to lead a Can-Can. The first was Josephine Baker, who had a show at The *Folies Bergère* in the 1920s. After I moved back to the United States I was asked if I hung out with Ms. Baker. I was age range Minus 40-fetus and apparently not the only person bad at math, so no. Moron. In the second draft of this manuscript I spelled Bergère wrong. This is why I got a D in French. Thanks a lot Johnny Carson.

One day Keith called our apartment but Lindy was out - probably running guns to the rebels in South America or whatever else she did in-between clarinet lessons - and Mom answered the phone. Keith was very polite, said he was calling for the "naughty stuff." Mom is French and her English comprehension, while mostly excellent, sometimes leaves a lot to be desired when other people have an accent. Like the English.

Suzy at La Nouvelle Eve in Paris

"Linzy, (Mom never used the D in my sister's name. And no, she's not Asian, she can pronounce them.) what eez zee naughty stuff?

"Uhhhh, you know, stuff people do in their homes."

"Like what?"

"Uhhhh, sex, stuff like that."
"A man named Keith called and asked for zat."
"WHAT?"
"He asked for zee naughty stuff. Who eez he?"
"He was just kidding, Mom."
"So he was asking you for zee sex?"
"OH DEAR GOD STOP TALKING."

While the Stones were in town that week, and after my last show at *La Nouvelle Eve*, (2 shows a night, 3 on the weekends), I headed over to their hotel to meet up with Lindy. I was a huge, obsessive fan of Jagger's and was hoping to meet him. Lindy was having dinner with them, plus Bianca Jagger, Anita Pallenberg, drummer Ollie Brown and piano player Billy Preston every night. I was beside myself with envy. Seriously, a picture of me taken in those days would reveal Regular Pasty-Skinned Suzy and standing next to her, Green Suzy.

One night I managed to meet up with them at a banquet. I got there late and didn't see Mick but spotted Bill Wyman, alone and unattended, my favorite way to ruin a celebrity's night. I approached him just as a guest at the dinner was about to take his picture. I asked if she'd take one with me and Bill. Then of course I had to ask Bill. He was always known as the "Ugly One" but up close he wasn't. He was actually very handsome; he just photographed badly. As we posed, the lady taking the Polaroid motioned me over and whispered that my top was completely see-through. So I held my grey purse across my boobs and look mental in the picture.

Another night I caught a large group of them as they returned from a restaurant.

Sidebar: Over the years I'd heard that Mick never pays for dinners anywhere, and Lindy confirmed that he didn't reach for his wallet the entire week she ate with them. Others did, but not Mick. She said the owner of whatever restaurant they were in always came to their table and personally gave him a pass.

We were all in the lobby and Mick walked towards me. I walked towards him, and we stopped when we came face to face. He smiled and said, "Hi."

Finally! A chance to talk to him. Discuss some music! Give him some ideas for titles since it had worked so well with Paul Anka! I took a deep breath and asked him where the ladies' room was.

Bill Wyman and me with my purse covering my boobs

***

On a trip to LA to hang out with Lindy, I met up with old friend Jack Scalia. Jack had successfully transitioned from modeling to movies and TV and was filming *The Devlin Connection*, co-starring Rock Hudson.

Rock Hudson, the biggest movie star of that time, was one of my earliest crushes. I'd seen every movie he did with Doris Day and had no idea he was gay. No one did.

Sidebar: The only other celebrities I'd met up until then were the Rolling Stones and Woody Allen. My dad took me to see Woody do stand-up, got us backstage, and asked for his autograph because HIS DAUGHTER WANTED TO BE A COMEDIAN OH MY GOD HE DID NOT JUST SAY THAT OUT LOUD AND I HOPE THERE AREN'T ANY BOYS LISTENING. When I was age range fetus-5, I met Phil Silvers, who played Sgt. Bilko on his eponymous show, on an ocean crossing to France. Both my sister and I got his autograph but I lost mine. So I have hers, framed. I'll pay you big money not to tell her. But first you're going to have to give me big money so I can pay you.

I asked Jack if I could meet Rock and he invited me to the set. I was a nervous wreck and from the moment I saw Rock, I was awestruck. He was so beautiful but not very talkative, or at least that's how I interpreted it. So I mistakenly took this as a sign to entertain him by being funny. (It's a sickness.) So I began a series of inane conversations that, later on, Lindy said were incomprehensibly stupid. (I'm pretty sure we were all drinking. Surprise!) It was so long ago that I've mercifully forgotten the exact bent of this hilarity. I only remember that Jack called me the next day and said, "What the FUCK was that about?"

***

One day, driving back to Hollywood from my sister's place in Santa Monica, I pulled up to a stop light. I looked in my rear-view mirror and saw ten black SUVs behind me, queued up like gamers waiting for the new PlayStation 3. That can only mean one of two things: paparazzi or bodyguards for someone really important. I glanced to my left and in the Mercedes next to me were Maria Shriver and Arnold Schwarzenegger.

I honked my horn and Maria turned towards me. I mouthed the words I LOVE YOU. She smiled and mouthed back THANK YOU. Then I nodded towards her husband and mouthed, NOT HIM. She must have laughed out loud since Arnold looked over at her and scowled. Thank God the light turned green and I took off. I did not need a state tax audit thank you very much.

Recently, when Arnold got popped for having slept with his housekeeper and fathering her child, our mutual friend Toni called Lindy and said Arnold was taking a beating in the press, and they should speak out on his behalf. Since they'd known him for over fifteen years, they knew a different side of him. Plus they'd hung out with him at World's Gym when he owned it. Toni insisted they help him out. But, like me, Lindy was Team Maria.

***

More movie and TV stars shop at Gelson's Market than anywhere else except possibly Malibu. It's over-priced and has terrible produce but it does have people watching. If they put a bar in and took the deli out, it would be the hottest place in town.

I'd recently seen the movie *You Can Count on Me* starring Laura Linney and Mark Ruffalo. It's a small movie but Linney and Ruffalo were astonishing. As I rounded the corner of the shamefully high-priced roasted chicken display case, there was Ruffalo. I was so surprised to see him that I said, "ohmygod I love you and have seen everything you've ever done." Skipped over my usual opening salvo and went straight to Stalkertown, California. And I hadn't seen everything he'd ever done. I'm amazed I even recognized him.

"Thanks," he said and stopped walking.

"I just saw you in…in…in… OH CRAP I'VE FORGOTTEN THE NAME OF IT BUT YOU WERE AMAZING!" Thankfully, he laughed.

"That's really nice of you to say."

At that point I realized he must have not been very famous because he was talking to me and not looking around for an escape route.

"I have to tell you, you're a LOT hotter in person."

That made him laugh and in my mind, decide to run away with me.

"Thank you, I really appreciate that."
"I'm not kidding; you are very, very hot."

And then everything got ruined. Because a small, evil child walked up to him and said, "Dad?" Dad! What kind of bullshit was this? Ruffalo reached out and took the interloper's small, probably sticky, hand.

"Well, we gotta go."
"Nice talking to you."
"Yeah, me too."

And so I had no option of becoming his future ex-wife.

Amazon Review by ArraysSnub: 5.0 out of 5 stars
Loved rock hudson loved doris day love the rolling stones love mark rufallo altho I;m not sure I know who he is and hate ahhnold.

Amazon Review by LieOneCoke: 5.0 out of 5 stars
As you can see by my name Im a big fan of keith Richard and god bless your sister for keeping him high and say high to her from me!

Author Suzy Soro's reply to LieOneCoke:
I will, as soon as she gets back from setting up underage garment factories in Uzbekistan.

Gone But Not Forgotten

There's a scene in *NewsRadio* when broadcaster Bill McNeal, played by Phil Hartman, walks down a flight of stairs to his office. Only he's not going down any stairs - he's walking in place and squatting down to make it appear like he's walking down a staircase. Bill's commitment to walking down those invisible stairs sums up the level of dedication Phil Hartman brought to any role he played. I would have sworn in a court of law that yes, there was a staircase present. And not any staircase: a down staircase.

Phil Hartman was a sweetheart. There really is no better way to describe him. That night at the LA Improv, when he asked Dennis Miller to come see my set to consider me for Dennis's new talk show, is an example of his kindness, his generosity. He was not jealous or competitive in any way, and that's rare in a town like Hollywood, where there's an estimated 110,000 actors. His friends were, and still are, intensely loyal. He was the kind of man that people would do a favor for in a New York minute. Later, Phil's wife, Brynn, told me that one of Dennis's children had been sick that night and after my gig he'd rushed home to Santa Barbara, almost two hours north of Los Angeles. But he didn't hesitate to do a favor for Phil.

Sidebar: Before Dennis left that night, he told Phil he'd like to see me again. That's normal in stand-up; people will see you over and over before they make a determination on whether you're in or you're out. It depends on your jokes and often whether you have any heat in the business. Before Dennis got a chance to see me again, his show was cancelled.

Dana Carvey, Phil Hartman and the man who reduced me to the third wheel: Brent Hollows

At Phil's fortieth birthday party he asked Jay Leno to put me on *The Tonight Show.* Jay was a big fan of Phil's, had even asked him, once he left *Saturday Night Live,* to be his permanent sidekick on the show. Phil declined.

"What kind of comedy do you do?" Jay asked me.

"Well, I'm sarcastic…" I began.

"That's not a type of comedy. What do you talk about, what are you sarcastic about?"

"My French mom, my trouble getting dates..." And then I stopped. Outside of being "sarcastic," I'd never broken down my type of comedy. Jay quickly lost interest and turned to talk to someone else. It was like being with my family at Thanksgiving, minus all the crying.

Jay had asked a stupid question. I'm pretty sure comedians aren't screened for the show based entirely on their subject matter. I'm sure being funny figures heavily into whether you get on the show or not. I think Jay was just blowing me off. Nice.

Wherever Phil went his fans stopped to talk to him and he never, ever, ignored them. Even when he was with his family in a public place, he made time to talk to anyone who approached him. He told me that he'd struggled for so long for some recognition that it was inconceivable for him to snub anyone who helped put him on the map. Unlike other celebrities who don't talk to fans, or wave off autographs and pictures, Phil did neither.

Phil was very creative and had impeccable taste. He designed album covers for bands like Poco and designed one of the logos for Crosby, Stills & Nash. He also designed Brynn's engagement ring after researching all the grades of diamonds and sapphires.

His creativity also showed in their home. Even though Brynn used a decorator, it was Phil who had the final say on whether something stayed or not. He was also up-to-date on fashion; once, when she brought home over-the-knee boots, he made her take them back because they were "too trendy."

One of the best Thanksgivings I ever had was with the Hartman's, at Dana Carvey's house. We were all seated at a long table, with Dana and his wife, Paula Zwaggerman, at one end and Brynn and Phil at the other. I was seated between Phil and comedian Mark Pitta. Across from me was Lindy and next to her was Jon Lovitz, and next to him was actor and comedian Kevin Pollak and his wife, Canadian comedian Lucy Webb. It was like being at the Emmy's, only with turkey.

With a table full of talent like that, I should have paid a cover charge to take part in it. At one point they took turns doing Jack Nicholson impressions. First Jon Lovitz, then Mark Pitta, then Kevin Pollak and lastly Phil. Only Dana, at the opposite end, did not join in. There was no winner, they were all incredible. Lindy, my permanent date for most of the Hartman events, (until she started dating Brent Hollows, whom she almost married, and then I became the third wheel and oh my how much fun is *that*?) and I sat transfixed.

Phil, Suzy, Brynn at the American Comedy Awards

After dinner we gathered around the Carvey's living room fireplace. I don't remember how the topic came up, whether it was a metaphysical discussion or just random blabbing, but Kevin Pollak told the most beautiful story about the love he felt for his wife, Lucy.

Sidebar: One weekend Brynn hired a psychic for her girlfriends. The psychic was strange, ethereal, otherworldly. The psychic set up in Brynn and Phil's bedroom and one by one we all had a consultation. When Brynn's turn came, she was gone a very long time. The next day I asked her why, and she replied that the psychic told her something so horrible that she broke down crying and couldn't stop. Brynn never offered up the story, at least not to me. I wish now I'd asked what it was. Lucy Webb was also at that psychic party and she and I got into a conversation about *Seinfeld*, which I'd recently shot. She said she was the original inspiration for the part of Elaine, something I'd never heard before. Many people think the character of Elaine was based on writer and comedian Carol Leifer, while others credit women who dated either Jerry or Larry. But no one mentioned Lucy. I asked her why it hadn't made any of the press and she said she didn't know but speculated someone at *Seinfeld* didn't want it revealed. There is no mention of it anywhere on the Internet.

As Kevin sat on the floor in front of the fireplace, he said he knew in his heart that the reason he was put on Earth, *the reason he was born*, was to take care of Lucy. It was so heartfelt. So touching. I thought how lucky it would be to have a man in my life who thought similarly, as opposed to the yahoos I attract who were put on this Earth to annoy me. Lindy and I talked about that speech for a long time afterward. How fortunate Lucy was. Where could we find a guy like that?

Kevin and Lucy are now divorced.

After Phil and Brynn died in 1998, the *National Enquirer* and the *Los Angeles Times* stalked me. The *Los Angeles Times* rang the intercom at my apartment building; when they announced themselves I hung up. They didn't come back. I wasn't so lucky with the *Enquirer*. They didn't come to my building but they called relentlessly. How did they know I was friends with the Hartmans? How did they get my phone number?

The day they died I drove to their home in Encino, a suburb of Los Angeles. I felt I had to be there even though their street was blocked off and there were cops everywhere. There was nothing I could do but I sat in my parked car, across Ventura Boulevard, crying.

Sidebar: My darling friend Brynn, in a moment of crazed addiction, shot her husband Phil Hartman. She then left the house and went to a friend's, confessing everything. High on drugs, she passed out. The next day, the friend asked her if the story was true and when she said it was, went back to her home with her. He called 911, the police arrived, removed the children from the house and as they did, Brynn barricaded herself in their master suite and shot herself, on their bed.

I couldn't see their house from my car but I sat there anyway. A man approached and asked if I was a fan. I said I was a friend. He asked if I knew anything about what happened. I said I didn't, rolled up my window, and drove away. What I never imagined was that the guy took down my license plate number, ran it, and found my address and phone number. Because that guy was a reporter.

The *Enquirer* left messages asking me to contact them; they'd pay for any information I could give them. I didn't call.

When Phil and Brynn first moved to New York, after Phil got *Saturday Night Live*, Lindy asked me to have lunch with Brynn – they were friends - because she didn't know anyone in NY and Phil was busy with the show. So I called and we met for lunch. I hoped we'd have something in common. I wish Lindy had mentioned Brynn was gorgeous, so I could have had time to have a face-lift and a new body installed before our lunch. She was the kind of woman who turned heads when she entered a room or walked down a street. And whereas I'd had a series of unremarkable men in my life, she had the exact opposite. She'd dated Rob Reiner before she met Phil. Intelligent, creative men were drawn to her, while I attract withholding narcissistic men. What were we going to talk about?

Plenty, as it turned out. Brynn was very funny. Her favorite thing was to call people and pretend she was Delores Hope, Bob

Hope's wife. It was funny because who the hell knew what Delores Hope sounded like? I was in Anchorage, Alaska, doing a week of shows and Brynn and Phil called to wish me a Happy Birthday. But they didn't know I was on the road so they sang to my answering machine. Brynn sang it as Delores Hope.

We both also had a madlydeeplycrazy crush on singer Dean Martin. For one of her birthdays I tracked down a vinyl copy of one of his albums. Of course neither of us had a turntable but that wasn't the point.

After they died, I got annoyed hearing all the nasty things said about Brynn. *I wasn't there. I wasn't in the relationship.* I've watched enough *Dateline NBC*s to know all is not what it appears, even to close friends and family.

I don't condone what Brynn did. And I'm not going to pretend it isn't difficult to witness a friend falling from grace but one thing I want to make perfectly clear, one thing all the papers and pundits were saying was totally out of line: that she couldn't have possibly loved her children to do what she did. That she was a bad mother. And nothing, and I mean *NOTHING*, could have been further from the truth. She loved those kids and was devoted to them.

Addiction is a horrible place to be in life and I know first-hand because I've been in rehab. When someone is in the grips of an addiction they are not in their right mind. Much has been written about comedian Andy Dick and how he got Brynn back into drugs. I don't believe anyone can "get you back into drugs" or any other addiction. There is a responsibility one assumes for one's behavior. The picture on the cover of this book of me and Andy was taken at the Hartman house, the night of a big party. At one point during the party I saw Brynn and Andy exit a bathroom together. Days later Brynn admitted they were doing coke.

Another thing never mentioned about Brynn was her incredible generosity. Both she and Phil were generous to a fault, but Brynn was always mindful of her friends who were broke. (Her best friend, Judy, and I were her two brokest friends.) Brynn and Phil would go to New York and Brynn would buy a new wardrobe.

When she got back to LA, she'd take all her old clothes and various swag-bag gifts and freebies Phil got from awards shows and lay them all out on the bed. Then she'd invite me over. I knew she was going to invite Judy over later but always told her to invite Judy first. After all, they were closer. And Brynn would laugh and say, "Yeah, but you're broker!" I got fabulous clothes from her, some hardly a year old. I still have some of the things she gave me.

If you went shopping with her and pointed out something you liked, as I did once with a silver ring covered with stars, it always ended up in the final tally only you didn't know it. Brynn would signal the clerk to add it and then later that afternoon, at lunch or cocktails, she'd present you with whatever it was you liked, in my case, the silver ring. Once she and Lindy went shopping and she picked out a necklace and shirt for me because I had a birthday coming up. If she invited people over for a catered Thanksgiving, every guest got a gift baggie of food to take home. The day after they died, my sister received a bracelet in the mail. It was from Brynn, for Lindy's birthday, which was six days prior to their deaths. If she went to the trouble to shop for Lindy's birthday, she clearly wasn't preparing to kill her husband. Or die.

Lindy hasn't taken the bracelet off since.

Why am I going on and on about Brynn? After all, what she did was unforgiveable in the eyes of the public, and especially in the eyes of Phil's adoring friends and fans. I'm going on and on because no one printed the good parts of Brynn. And there were good parts. And she has children, and even though many of us have told them how wonderful both their parents were, it's important to me to fill in some of the blanks in her story. I'd hope someone would do that for me if the occasion arose.

One day, on the phone with Lindy, I mentioned the *National Enquirer* wouldn't stop calling me, that they wanted me to sell them a story on Brynn. Lindy repeated the story to our friend Toni, also a friend of Brynn's. One day Toni and her sister Lori did a conference call with me.

"You should sell the *Enquirer* your story," Lori said.

Tony added, "You know Brynn wouldn't care. She'd want you to make some money if you could."

"But I would never tell them anything bad about her. She was a wonderful woman."

"Then don't."

"Well why would they pay me to hear a bunch of nice things about her?"

"They wouldn't."

"I'm not following."

"They don't know what you're going to say, so pretend you have some dish for them," Toni said. Toni was always the mastermind of our group.

Sidebar: Toni was also the person who asked Lindy to come forward with her and say nice things about Arnold Schwarzenegger when it was discovered he'd fathered a child with his housekeeper. Still Team Maria, Toni!

"How much did they offer to pay you?" Lori asked.

"$2,500."

"Holy shit, DO IT."

"Seriously, Suzy, you're an actress, act like you have something bad to say."

"Get the check first," Toni said.

So that's what happened. I made an appointment to meet with the reporters at the *Enquirer* in their offices on Sunset Boulevard. I even brought some pictures I had. (I regretted it later, as they never returned them to me.) They ushered me into a small room with a desk. I asked for the check and they handed it over. I wished I could cash it with my mind and send it straight to my bank account. After all, does anyone trust the *National Enquirer*?

"So what was your impression of Brynn?" the female reporter asked me.

"She was a lovely girl. Kind, beautiful, generous, and a wonderful mom."

"Well there must have something you noticed that wasn't normal."

"Well, she used to have Thanksgiving catered. That wasn't

normal. A lot of people cook, but not Brynn!"

"Was that because she was lazy?"

"No, not at all. She liked spending time with her guests, not being locked up in a kitchen slaving over a hot stove. And she could afford it so why not?"

"Nobody commented on Thanksgiving being catered?"

"Not until she had the caterers take all the leftovers and divvy them up for the guests when they left."

"Was she prone to violence?"

"Oh God no."

"But she had guns in the house. Obviously something was off there."

"Brynn had guns because they lived in a house with no security gate. One day she answered the door to some of Phil's fans who were hoping to meet him. That scared her, that people had such easy access to her home and children. After that she turned their master suite into a fortress, with the ability to lock it from the inside."

The interview went on for forty minutes. Because I was so emotional over their loss, I cried frequently. I think that's probably the only reason the reporter didn't yell at me or tell me to stop fucking around.

I waited for the *Enquirer* to hit newsstands. There wasn't a word of my interview in it. Not the next week or the week after that. Or ever. That's how evil the tabloids are. They have no interest in anything decent that pertains to a celebrity.

Sidebar: During the aftermath of their deaths, a former New York friend called out of the blue, asking me questions about Brynn and Phil. Since she also had also known Brynn I thought she was asking because she cared about them. I told her only what I knew. But when she called three days in a row, I remembered an old story I'd heard about her and her sister, that they used to sell information to the tabloids, they'd been doing it for years. I screened my calls from then on. Assholes.

But didn't this make me an asshole too? Isn't that what I'd done? Sell something for cash? I prefer to look at it as vindication for all the celebrities the *Enquirer* has vilified over the years. Including Brynn.

Amazon review by BanteringHarm: 4.0 out of 5 stars
I think it's great that you stuck up for your friend, despite what happened and what she did. None of us can judge each other because there but for the grace of...

Amazon review by AFamousPerson: 5.0 out of 5 stars
I'm glad someone screwed the Enquirer. Why not you?

Author Suzy Soro's reply to BanteringHarm:
I did it for her friends, and more importantly, for her children. Even though her children never knew I stuck up for her, they will now. And will hopefully forgive us both.

No Wonder Everybody Loves Her

During a week at the Last Laugh Comedy Club in Phoenix, Arizona, I shared a condo with a married comedian who had a girlfriend on the side. If he wasn't around when one of them called, I'd tell the wife or the girlfriend he was at a movie, when in reality he was with one of the waitresses – Tiffany, Krystal, Angel or another stripper name - from the comedy club. This was standard behavior among the male comics, covering for each other. I did the same because I didn't want to be that female comic who ruined everything with her judgments. There were already a lot of them the male comics complained about, refused to work with, even.

Sidebar: Comics stay in condos for the Tuesday-through- Sunday week they're on the road: disgusting, badly furnished maid-free condominiums leased or owned by comedy club owners. They're affectionately called comedy condos only there's nothing affectionate about them. For example, the mayonnaise in the fridge is not mayo because one guy, a long time ago, (because who else but a guy would think of it), traded out the mayo for something a little more *personal*.

The cheating comic spent a lot of time on the phone with his wife and one day I overheard his side of one of their conversations.

"No, not at all."
"I swear, really bad."
"Scottie Pippen."

I didn't think too much about it until the next day when she called back, her husband was out, and I answered. She asked me so many personal questions I felt like I was being vetted by Republicans for a Cabinet position in a Democratic administration. To get her off the phone I mentioned I was going to be on a TV show that night and that she should watch.

The following night the married comic yelled at me for telling his wife to watch me on TV.

"Why?"

"Because I told her you looked like Scottie Pippen."

If you were ever a fan of the Chicago Bulls, you'll remember Scottie Pippen was the one who looked least like Halle Berry.

This same married comic later came into my room at 3:00 a.m., while I was sleeping, and tapped me on the shoulder. When I woke up, he was holding a bottle of vodka and standing six inches from my head, wearing nothing but a towel. And it wasn't the way Ferris Beuhler wore it, around his head. I yelled at him to get out.

"Why did you come into my room last night?"

"I thought you might be thirsty."

"Thirsty? While I slept? And for vodka? Are you crazy?"

"I'm sorry."

From then on, when I lived with male comics in condos, I locked the door of my bedroom. Up until that time I'd never had to. I trusted them not to try and rape me. We were all on the front lines of a difficult profession, all on the same team, with the same problems, complaints, and heartbreaks. I now understood why Rosie O'Donnell refused to stay in condos.

Every afternoon in whatever condo in whatever town I was in, I watched *Oprah*. I had the remote in a death grip when that hour rolled around, because if one of the male comics got it, I'd have to watch 100 hours of basketball/baseball/football/scrambled porn.

TUESDAY
"What are you watching?"
"Oprah."
"Oprah? That's bullshit."

WEDNESDAY
"What are you watching?"
"Oprah."
"Again?"

THURSDAY
"Hey Suzy, you're going to miss Oprah."
"Thanks."

FRIDAY
"Suzy, Oprah's on, and *holy crap* Tom Cruise is jumping on her couch!"

SATURDAY
One hundred hours of basketball/baseball/football/scrambled porn.

SUNDAY
See Saturday.

I met Oprah Winfrey on the set of the movie *Indecent Proposal,* starring Robert Redford, Demi Moore, Woody Harrelson, and Billy Connolly. She was there to film Demi Moore for an upcoming show she was doing about her. I was a glorified extra with no lines, hired by Director Adrian Lyne to 'help' the stars of the movie. Adrian, who also directed *Fatal Attraction* and *Flashdance,* hired six comedians to make the stars of the movie laugh before they did their scenes, thereby making them more relaxed. I guess the film budget wasn't big enough to hire masseurs.

The shoot lasted a few days for the day-players. Two of the comedians left, deciding it was demeaning to stand around and be funny for day-player money. I'll take any money to be on a movie set with Robert Redford. Even Canadian. Sorry, Canada.

Robert Redford never mingled with the other actors or the crew. He ate his meals in his trailer. So a few of us would stand around waiting for him to walk by, and by a few of us, I mean me. I knew I could get him to talk to me, possibly even marry me, once he got past all my crazy parts which admittedly would take a very long time.

So one day when we all broke for lunch I saw him heading off alone to his trailer.

"Hey, Mr. Redford!" I yelled. He stopped walking and turned around.

"How come you never eat with the cast?"

"WHY ARE YOU TALKING TO ME I'M A BIG STAR."

Sidebar: This has been Suzy Soro reporting for Hyperbole News Network.

He said he preferred to eat alone so he could learn his lines for upcoming scenes. What kind of *crazy* acting preparation was that?

The next day Oprah was walking away from Redford's trailer and of course I threw myself in front of her. Turns out she'd asked Redford if he'd be interviewed for the segment on Moore but he turned her down. She rolled her eyes and said, "He's a bigger star than Demi, just in case we all forgot."

Then I told her the story of the male comics in the condo and how eventually they all ended up watching her show with me. She laughed.

Later that same day, when we were all on set, she was watching the scene we were shooting. I looked over at her and she waved. I turned to see who she was waving at but there was no one there. I looked at her again and she waved again and once more I looked behind me. There was no one there. I looked back at Oprah and she waved and pointed to me over and over.

Finally I got it and waved back. Pretty sure she rolled her eyes.

Amazon Review by PINPOETICPEST: 4.0 out of 5 stars
As a fan of the Championship Chicago Bulls I find it offensive that you would refer to Scottie Pippen's looks over his basketball skills.

Author Suzy Soro's reply to PINPOETICPEST:
As a fan of the Championship Oprah Winfrey Show I find it offensive that you never saw Tom Cruise jump on her couch.

Tall, Dark, and Funny

The first time I met comedian David Brenner was at Xenon, a club in New York City now long gone. He was standing alone at the edge of the dance floor, watching people dance. I walked over and stood next to him and pretended I was watching people dance. I was very nervous. David was a big star in the stand-up comedy world and was always guest-hosting *The Tonight Show*.

It was the 80s and everyone in the club was wearing shoulder pads. I didn't really need them so I looked like a linebacker, which had been frightening away men for years. I wasn't aware of this because the 80s = Quaalude addiction and transitioning from gin to vodka. I was never sober long enough to notice men asking me to pass them the ball as they ran down the field into the arms of a Barbie.

I made a comment about the people dancing and he laughed. So I took this as a marriage proposal and struck up a one-sided conversation, my spécialité de la maison. He was incredibly nice and very funny and we went back and forth for about fifteen minutes, me trying desperately to make him laugh with every sentence. (See Rock Hudson story.) (Also see Johnny Carson story.) (It's a sickness.)

Then I noticed my boyfriend glaring at me and I ended the conversation. As I walked away David said, "You should do stand-up. Contact my agent, Artie Moskowitz, at the William Morris Agency, and mention my name." I was naïve back then and thought I had about a hundred years to come up with an act, and that William Morris would automatically accept my calls at any time in the future. Meanwhile, I had no act, and more importantly, wasn't even a stand-up comic

Sidebar: Like with Johnny Carson, right person, wrong time. Doubly ironic if you're a comic.

David comes from the generation of comedians that were really, really famous. They got that way without the help of reality TV or HBO specials. They didn't need the comedy boom of the 80s to help them either, because they were working steadily long before that.

Many years later David and I met again on the New York set of *Every Day with Joan Lunden*, a talk show Joan had after she left *Good Morning America*. I was booked to do a five minute stand-up set and as luck would have it, David was the guest co-host. Talk shows are impossibly difficult to do since the studio audience isn't being served alcohol, which someone really needs to look into. But I heard Brenner laughing behind me and that's what kept me going.

I then ran into him years later when he was doing a run-through for his own game show here in LA, and I was booked as one of the practice contestants. Before game shows are released, there are many rehearsals with actors filling in as contestants. In this case, the people they used were comedians. The premise of the show was that David's 'assistant' sat at a desk next to the host's (David's)podium and interrupts him with scheduling questions, phone calls, and dinner reservations, all while David hosts a game show. It was one of the cleverer game show premises because David got to be funny, and the 'assistant' got to be annoying. And there were prizes!

At one point the director yelled 'Cut' and David announced to the crew and the other comics that he had worked with me before and that I was funny. Earlier, I'd reminded him that we had done Lunden's show together, but he didn't have to make that comment; it was a nice thing to do.

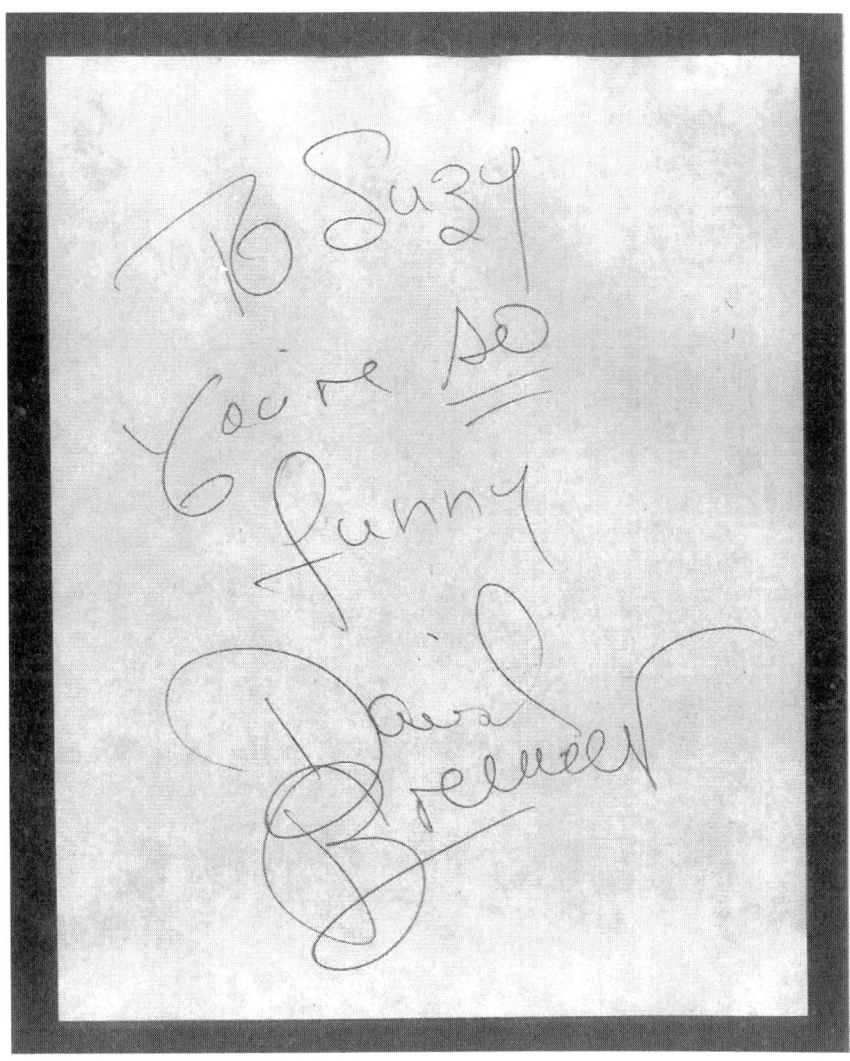

I did an interview with David for my blog back in 2007, and the following is excerpted from it:

SUZY: You hold the record for the most appearances on *The*

Tonight Show and also for *The Mike Douglas Show*, and have been a guest on more talk shows than any entertainer in the history of TV.

DAVID: "It's nice to hold such records, but let me tell you what it is really worth. If after performing a show I were to invite everyone in the audience to join me at a nearby bar for drinks on me, and after we all drank and had some laughs I went up to the cashier and said, "I hold the record for the most appearances on *The Tonight Show, Mike Douglas,* and have been a guest on more talk shows than anyone else," she would reply, "That'll be $895.00, sir.""

These are some of my favorite stories about how David ran his stand-up career when times were bleak:

DAVID: "I had been the opening act for Sonny and Cher from the time we first worked together at the Sahara Hotel in Vegas in 1971, when they were trying to make a comeback, right through their very last show together. The sudden demise of this hot duo left me with very little work booked for the remaining nine months of the year. In order to not drop off the monetary map (go broke) I walked into my agent's office, told him to put my ego in the bottom drawer of his desk and lower my price for one nighters and weekly gigs, figuring that when buyers could hire me for the same price as comedians not as popular, I'd get the gigs. It worked. On January 1 of the next year, my agent gave me back my ego and I raised my prices higher than they had ever been, which also worked."

"After a few years of being the co-headliner in Vegas, I had offers from many of the hotels/casinos to be their exclusive headliner, based on estimations of my drawing 900 customers a show, often filling more seats than the headliners. Headliners made more money, as much as 25% more. Maybe even more appealing, their names were on the top of the marquee and they were called 'Headliners.' Once again, I put my ego in a bottom drawer and remained a co-headliner. Why? Let's say the headliner earned

$100,000 a week and the co-headliner got only $75,000 (which is far from 'only.') The headliner's exclusive contract called for six or eight weeks a year = $600,000 or $800,000 a year. I freelanced, worked all the hotels, mostly hired by headliners who knew I guaranteed them full houses for which they got all the credit. For over a decade, I averaged a yearly twenty to twenty-five weeks of work = $1,500,000 or $1,875,000 a year, so, bullshit titles & marquee placement aside, who made more money in Vegas?"

***

After the run-through for David's game show I asked him to sign my copy of his book, *People Never See You Eat Tuna Fish*. I clutched it in a death grip all the way back to the parking lot. I was afraid to open it in case it was a bland, 'Best Wishes, David' inscription, which would have been fine. But you know, not really.

I sat in my grey Ford Festiva age range cheap-decrepit, *even with red racing stripes* - and opened the cover. He'd written: *To Suzy, you are so funny.* Male comics are not that charitable when they refer to female comics. Most of them don't think we're funny. If you ask a male comic to list his favorite female comic he'll hesitate, then name the one who isn't funny but is a Hollywood Darling. I'll let you figure out who I'm talking about. David's inscribed note was the first compliment I'd ever gotten from a male comic. David is a class act and remains one of the most positive and generous comics I've ever known. The last time we worked together was for a variety show that was in pre-production in Miami. I was the head writer and often spoke with David, who was in NY, since he was the host. Eventually the Executive Producer of the show stole all the money, took his coke stash, and headed for parts unknown.

Amazon review by SillierSnore: 2.0 out of 5 stars
This woman is so self serving she can't wait to mention how funny she is.

Author Suzy Soro's reply to SillierSnore:
You're right.

Amazon review by VastMadBit: 2.0 out of 5 stars
I could have saved myself the cost of this book by just reading her blog. Why do book publishers always give bloggers book deals and think they're good writers?

Author Suzy Soro's reply to VastMadBit:
I give up, why?

The Good, the Fat, and the Free Husband

At the cashier's at Victor's Restaurant in the Hollywood Hills, I was in line ahead of actress Kathy Baker, who was with a younger man. She was holding her bill and her credit card and was obviously going to pay for their meal. I thought, of course she is. That's the thing about everyone knowing you have more money than the guy you're eating lunch with - who you don't recognize from film or TV and if you don't recognize him then he's not famous - you know Old Kath has to foot the bill. I told her she was brilliant and I watched everything she did on TV. I said I missed seeing her on the show *Picket Fences* and I wished she would do another series. When was she going to return to TV? She said she was currently on the show *Boston Public*.

I don't know why I bother.

***

There was only one time I wanted to hurt a celebrity and that celebrity was Conchata Ferrell, the woman who plays Berta on both versions of *Two and a Half Men,* the one with Charlie Sheen and the one that isn't funny.

I was at Arclight Cinema in Hollywood, where tickets cost $16, ($19.50 if the film is in 3-D) but you can reserve a seat in a specific row and get a more refined and up-market crowd. I'd rather push and shove through a crowd of gang-bangers brandishing semi-automatic weapons and only pay $8, but maybe that's just me. Celebrities from Tom Hanks to Charlize Theron let you bother them. And by you I think we all know I mean me. I once had an entire conversation with Georgia Engel (Georgette on *Mary Tyler Moore* and Robert's mother-in-law on *Everybody Loves Raymond*) while she peed and I lurked outside her stall. I really should have apologized for that.

I was at the tail end of recovering from ankle surgery and still using a cane to get around when I went to Arclight to see *Catfish*. When the film ended, I made my way over to the stairs and used my cane to negotiate one cautious step at a time. I walked slowly so I wouldn't pitch headlong into the people in front of me. Suddenly I heard a rather stern "Uh, exCUUSE me." I turned in time to see Conchata, an incredibly large woman, looming over me. She was walking next to her painfully thin husband, who dutifully stayed by her side as she lumbered down the stairs, attempting to overtake me. He was the velociraptor to her T-Rex and I was Newman from *Seinfeld*, waiting in that jeep to get eaten. Remember when everyone thought fat people were jolly? When did that end? Or did it only apply to Santa Claus?

I stopped hobbling and leaned into the railing, nearly getting smothered as she passed by. It was obvious I was using a cane; it was in plain sight. What was Conchata in such a hurry for? An extra minute, tops, and I would reach the bottom of the stairs and then she could pass me. Once down in the lobby I caught up with her and her husband and passed them. All that drama on the stairs for me to eventually overtake her in the lobby. Bitch.

***

I was in New York in 1994, preparing to film a segment of *Girl's Night Out*, a showcase for female stand-up comics. The host for my show was Anne Meara, actor Ben Stiller's mom and character actor Jerry Stiller's wife.

Sidebar: Stiller and Meara were one of the top comedy teams in the 60s and 70s. More recently, Stiller played Jerry's father on

Seinfeld, and Meara is best remembered as Miranda's mother-in-law on *Sex and the City*. They currently have a web series on Hulu.com called *Stiller and Meara*.

    Anne and I were getting hair and makeup at the same time.
    "You're so lucky; you have a great career and a great marriage."
    "Thanks."
    "What's the secret to your marriage?"
    "Therapy. Lots and lots of therapy."
    "Jerry seems like a good guy."
    "You want him?"

Amazon review by BratsEbb: 4.0 out of 5 stars
I remember Jerry stiller from The king of Queens, that show about gay UPS drivers. Maybe your thinking of Nichols and may? I think they were around in the 50s.

Author Suzy Soro's reply to BratsEbb:
I stand corrected. Using a cane, of course.

It's The Only Reason I Watch The Oscars

I was sitting in my car at a stoplight on Sunset Boulevard when someone honked. It's illegal to honk in Los Angeles. You can buy crystal meth on a street corner but if you honk to get the dealer's attention, we'll see you in court. It should be legal to honk because Los Angeles has very questionable motorists who do everything but drive when they're behind the wheel of a vehicle. Talking on their cell, combing their hair, putting on mascara? Amateurs. I saw a driver in a convertible making an origami crane while he waited for his cordless Panini maker to finish. From then on I started driving defensively, meaning scared stiff. The one and only time I was hit by a car in L. A. I was standing in the bedroom. Of a hotel. On the 2nd floor.

Sidebar: This is Suzy Soro reporting for Hyperbole News Network.

Okay, the truth is that I *was* hit by a car. While crossing a street. On foot. I fell backwards on my hair barrette and the guy who hit me jumped out of his car and asked if he could take me to the hospital. It was all I could do not to reply, "Can we stop at a beauty supply on the way?"

Another car honk.

I glanced in my rear view mirror. A man sitting in a red Honda was staring at his lap. It looked like he was eating a French fry. He kept staring at his lap while his hand dipped down and ohmygod what was he doing, feeding his penis carbohydrates? Carbs put on weight in the thighs and stomach area but will not help with penis enlargement, at least not according to the emails I get. As I continued staring in my rear view, I saw that the French fry was actually a pencil and when he held up a slab of newspaper, realized he was doing a crossword puzzle. Sure, what better place than in bumper to bumper traffic - while you're eating?

The unknown driver honked more impatiently now, three quick bursts. I glanced to my left and then to my right, and there was Dinah Shore sitting in her car. At least it looked like her, the short blond helmet of hair, the toothy grin. But wasn't Dinah dead? I tried to remember if I'd ever seen her on an Academy Awards death reel. Or maybe the one on the Emmy's? Without those death reels I'm at a loss for trivial cocktail party patter. Let's see, after Dinah Shore stopped dating Burt Reynolds, whenever that was, I stopped paying attention to her life. I didn't even know if Burt Reynolds was still alive. He's one of those people who will eventually appear on the death reel at the Academy Awards and people will remark, "I thought he was already dead."

Then the woman who I thought might be Dinah Shore fluttered her fingers and Yoo Hooed me. And I finally placed her: it was Dr. Joyce Brothers. All those women from the 50s and 60s had the Stepford Wife Shellacked Bouffant. No wonder I was confused.

"Excuse me dear, do you know where the Street-I'd-Never-Heard-Of is?"

"I contemplated telling her about my dysfunctional childhood at the hands of a narcissistic mother and an emotionally vacant father, after all, she was a shrink, but instead said, "Straight ahead."

"Just straight ahead?"

"It's a whole bunch of stoplights, but yeah."

She thanked me, stepped on the gas and drove off.

I kept driving but never passed the Street-I'd-Never-Heard-Of. I'd given Dr. Brothers the wrong information; if she listened to me she'd be on her way to Vegas in about nineteen stoplights.

And for the record, I'm not a big fan of Dr. Joyce Brothers, I don't really think she's a celebrity, and I'm unclear as to whether or not she's still alive. I'll have to keep watching the Oscars and get back to you on that.

Amazon review by JuryNail: 3.0 out of 4 stars
I remember Dr. Joyce Brothers. I think she had a newspaper column and was like Dear Abby. Although I might be thinking of Dear Abby. Ann Landers? Maybe I don't remember Dr. Brothers.

Author Suzy Soro's reply to JuryNail:
She had weird capped teeth. No one in LA has weird capped teeth and isn't in show business. I might be thinking of Dinah Shore though.

The Five Ds

One weekend I was booked to do shows at Vandenberg Air Force Base and the following weekend, at Edwards Air Force Base. Danny Woodburn, who played Mickey on *Seinfeld*, was on the bill with me, along with another male comic whose name I've forgotten. It's okay, he's probably forgotten mine.

Danny's a Little Person. Not a dwarf. Probably because The Dwarves are a rock band, or from a Tolkien novel about middle Earth, and I can understand not wanting to be lumped into that category. And not a midget, because if you call him that, congratulations, you've just used the N word for little people. Now run for your life.

Military shows can be a nightmare. Normally I would love a chance to be around so many men but I know from touring with Army MWR (Morale, Welfare and Recreation), and the USO, that soldiers are a schizy audience. Taking orders from superior officers, wearing the same thing day after day, it's like being a child again. They're never in control, so when they get to a comedy show, they go crazy and their first thought is to get control back from a comedian. And since some of these people have access to weapons of mass destruction, it's better if you don't yell at them. Military people love dirty jokes and comics who swear so naturally we're advised not to be dirty and not to swear.

Danny opened the show. I waited backstage and at first all I heard was him doing his act. Then the noise level rose considerably. And it was coming from the audience. They were heckling him. The stage manager ran backstage.

"They're fucking with the dwarf."

"What?"

"THEY'RE FUCKING WITH THE DWARF."

"You're supposed to call them Little People."

"I don't give a shit what you're supposed to call them, they're fucking with him and they're going to fuck with you too, so be prepared."

How to tell this guy there is no preparation for being "fucked with." Audiences are not hurricanes. You can't buy batteries and flashlights and board up your act. You can't put tape over your jokes and out on stage you go. Prepared!

Sidebar: Tennis ace John McEnroe once told me he couldn't believe the heckling comedians had to put up with, people shouting out hateful things and constantly interrupting the show.

"People always yell mean stuff at you when you play; it's the same thing."

"Oh, I don't hear any of that; I just focus on the game."

When my name was called I walked out on stage, picked up the mic, and bellowed, "Don't fuck with me, people, because I'm originally from New York and I'll take you motherfuckers *OUT*."

And they didn't fuck with me. After the show Danny just shrugged while I droned on and on about how badly the audience behaved. He's a much bigger person than I am.

***

One of my girlfriends, who lived in my old apartment building, started dating actor Dennis Quaid after he and Meg Ryan divorced. Their picture soon appeared on the cover of a tabloid and Meg reprimanded Dennis for it. Instead of bothering her ex, Meg should have spent time redoing her lip plastic surgery and getting them back to human size.

At the same time my girlfriend was dating Dennis, I was dating a man who lived out of town and only occasionally came into LA.

One weekend both the guy I was dating and Dennis were visiting. My girlfriend asked if I had any weed. I didn't. I'm that person who never buys it, then finds occasion to smoke, cleans out the nearest fridge, gains three pounds in a half an hour and doesn't smoke again for five years. But the man I was dating always had pot so I told her we'd come by later. I put on a lacy black teddy, thigh-high black silk stockings, elbow length black gloves and waited for my boyfriend to arrive.

Sidebar: I'm hoping my mother hasn't read this far in the book.

"We're going down to the first floor. Dennis Quaid is visiting."

"Dennis Quaid? I love Quaid. I've seen all his movies. What's he doing in your building?"

"He's visiting my friend; they're dating. Let's go."

"You're going like that?"

"Oh, right." I slipped on a coat, removed my elbow gloves, but left my pheromones on.

The crowd at my girlfriend's made the atmosphere feel like a zoo event, where the public is invited to see Dennis, the first movie star born in captivity, i.e. our rundown apartment building in the Hollywood Hills. He had a big bottle of Grey Goose and was pouring. Joints were passed around. Music played. My guy got into a conversation with him about one of his movies. They were talking shop while I nudged my girlfriend and gave her the knowing side eye. And then Dennis stood up and started to dance. And even though white men usually dance while doing the white man's overbite, Dennis didn't have that problem. That boy could dance.

The next day my guy called on his way out of town. "So I guess you're going to start dating Dennis Quaid now." I'm sorry, *what?*

"Did you *not* notice how beautiful my girlfriend is?"
"Yeah, but you still might go out with him."
"Uhhhh, don't you think Dennis might have a say in that?"

Me and Paul Dooley outside a movie theater

While it's flattering to think he thought Dennis would go out with me, it's not flattering that he thought I'd break up with him for Dennis. I really don't understand men at all. Especially the jealous ones. No, actually, none of them. And for the record, Johnny Jealous and I are no longer together. And Dennis Quaid and my girlfriend are now married. To other people.

***

Paul Dooley is one of Hollywood's best known character actors. His biggest role, the one that put him on the map, was as Ray, the father in the movie *Breaking Away*. But he is also the co-founder of the ground-breaking 1970s TV show *The Electric Company*. He also spent early years as a clown and a stand-up. The man has some serious chops.

Sidebar: Dennis Quaid was also in *Breaking Away*. After reading this book, my best friend Dennison said so many people appeared and reappeared in different stories of my life that the book should have been called Six Degrees of Suzy Soro.

Paul's range is so vast he's appeared in everything from *Law and Order, E.R., Sisters,* and *Star Trek: Deep Space Nine*. He's the guy who appears on screen and everyone goes, "Oh, it's THAT guy; I know that guy." That's the biggest compliment a character actor gets. So when Dennison did a play with him and Bea Arthur, *Afterplay*, I wanted to meet him.

Sidebar: See? Six degrees.

When I finally met him I was pleasantly surprised because he's very funny. And so is his wife, Winnie Holzman. She's the creator of *My So Called Life* and wrote the book for a little musical called *Wicked*. She was also a writer on *Once and Again and Thirtysomething*.

Dennison and I have film dates with Paul and Winnie because we all love to dissect movies. Ad nauseum. Last Christmas we went to see *The Sound of Her Voice*, a movie they were dying to see and one that Dennison and I had never heard of. Winnie and I sat next to each other at Arclight Cinema and immediately started chatting. People who pay $16 per ticket do not expect chatting. Good luck with me in the audience. Winnie told me a story about Larry David, how she'd called to invite him to be a guest speaker with her at an event and how she was put on hold for a very long time.

Sidebar: See? More six degrees.

"Were you on hold for long?" Larry asked when he finally picked up the line.

"Yeah, but no big deal."

"Is the song they play on the hold music the theme from *Friends*?"

"Yes."

"I hate that song."

Winnie and I continued blabbing about writing, actors, movies, and everything else Hollywood. We weren't watching the trailers. The trailers were nowhere near as interesting as Winnie Holzman. She's had as incredible a career as her husband. And their relationship, to me, was an amazing one. Both are in the arts, successful, and heavily respected. And in love. It's a success story the press ignores because no one gets humiliated or cheated on. All of a sudden Winnie turned to her left, where Paul was sitting.

"You need to stop talking," Paul whispered.

"It's only the trailers."

"It's disrespectful. You need to stop."

That's when I stopped eavesdropping and if you know me at all, you know that's as difficult for me as giving up refined sugar. They finished their sotto voce conversation and I slunk down in my seat, feeling like a five year-old. PAUL DOOLEY YELLED AT ME BY PROXY. Take that, Munchausen people.

The next time Dennison and I met them was to see *The Hunger Games*. I sat next to Paul and Winnie was exiled to an outer seat. I missed her.

***

During my days in Malibu, I spent hours wandering in and out of the boutiques at Cross Creek Mall, wishing their prices were lower. Across the highway from the mall is a Ralph's grocery store. I also spent a lot of time in there wishing their prices were lower.

One day I spotted Dick Van Dyke, the last person I expected to see at a supermarket. Like the time I ran into Angelina Jolie at Gelson's, I can't believe famous actors don't have people who food shop for them. I refuse to wrap my head around the fact that people who have reached their level of fame do normal activities. Because really normal people, like me, would give a right arm not to food shop, do laundry or dust. If I had the money I'd have someone sleep for me. Okay, maybe not a right arm, but definitely a toe, preferably one that isn't integral to that whole walking thing.

Sidebar: On the set of the movie *Silkwood*, starring Cher and Meryl Streep, Meryl ironed her own clothes. This drove Cher nuts and one day she asked Meryl why she didn't have "her people" do that for her. Meryl replied that it kept her grounded, to do her own ironing. Grounded? So in case of a lightening strike she'd be spared because she was holding an iron? I read that the Duchess of Cambridge does her own food shopping. *Dear Duchess, You're doing the Duchess gig wrong.* These people make me weep. If part of celebrity-hood does not involve getting others to do menial tasks for you why not just become a librarian and leave those open acting/duchessing spots available for the rest of us?

Dick Van Dyke is one of the only comedic actors to get his hand and footprints immortalized at Grauman's Chinese Theater on Hollywood Boulevard. He also has five Emmys, a Tony, and a Grammy. I once got a blue ribbon at day camp for not whining for an entire day.

I was going into Ralph's and Dick was exiting. And he was walking very fast. Which meant I had to walk faster if I was going to make this one of the most annoying days of his existence.

"Mr. Van Dyke?" He turned around.

"Hi," I said, "I'm a huge fan of yours."

"Thanks," Van Dyke said as he continued walking.

"*The Dick Van Dyke Show* was my favorite TV show."

"Mine too."

Oh my God we're dating!

"Your comedy was so inspired, and the writing is timeless."

"Thanks."

"I'm a comedian, too."

And there it was. The most ridiculous statement I could make to a master of comedy like Dick Van Dyke. It was like when I told Angelina Jolie's assistant that "I was in show business too." And as it came blowing out of my mouth, I touched Van Dyke on the arm, the universal sign for I'd like to have sex with you.

Van Dyke looked at me, then down at my hand. He even stopped walking. I removed my hand and smiled stupidly, pretending I touched his arm in some universal grand plan to get myself arrested by the crack security team at Ralph's.

"Well, good luck with your comedy," Van Dyke finally said.

"Thanks," I replied. We both turned and went in opposite directions. I didn't look back but I'm sure he was walking very fast.

***

I'd never seen a car like it, sleek, silver, low to the ground, and I couldn't stop staring at it, even when the driver got out of the car and walked towards the store. I nearly bumped into him as we met up at the same time at the entrance of Gelson's Market.

"Excuse me, what kind of car is that?"

"It's a…"

"Oh my *GOD*, you're Patrick…"

Patrick who? Stewart? No, this guy was not bald. Patrick Ewing? No, this guy was not black. Patrick Swayze? No, this guy was not dead.

It was McDreamy from *Grey's Anatomy*. I instantly memorized him. He had on a tight, navy blue ribbed sweater and a matching skull-cap knit hat. And jeans. Really nice, butt-hugging jeans. I was staring at him so hard I could see clear through to his brain and watched his synapses fire.

"I love your show," I said as he started walking (running) away from me.

"Thank you, very kind," he said turning left (breaking into a full gallop) into produce. He eats produce. How cool is *that*?

"Truly great show."

"Much appreciated," he launched over his shoulder as he rounded a corner and dropped out of sight.

I've said something meaningless and ridiculous to many off-brand celebrities in Gelson's over the years. Robert Pastorelli, the painter from *Murphy Brown* who died of a heroin overdose in 2004, right when he was being investigated for the death of his girlfriend; Gil Bellowes, Billy from *Ally McBeal*, who was killed off in a courtroom scene and up close has really bad skin; Aisha Tyler, currently one of the hosts of *The Talk,* and Alex Kingston, from *E.R.,* who claimed her contract wasn't renewed because she got too old and in this town, that's not hard to believe.

Alex looked genuinely frightened of me. So I started talking more and her eyes swept the entirety of the store a hundred times, probably searching for an exit. But Patrick Dempsey? Not an off-brand celebrity. He's short though. And I never did find out what kind of car he drove.

Amazon review by BadNeedierSnob: 4.0 out of 5 stars
Loved this chapter but can't find your CV attached like you said in the story about the dwarf.

Author Suzy Soro reply to BadNeedierSnob:
The little person.

American Idol

When I was age range 29-29 I moved to Los Angeles and got an agent, OmniPop, my former booking agents from New York. They'd opened a branch of their agency in LA and one of the first things they recommended was to call Jann Rowe at the American Comedy Awards to see if I could get myself invited to the annual event. They thought there was an off-chance she'd put me on the list but not to count on it as it was late to be calling for an invitation, and she didn't know who I was.

Jann worked for George Schlatter, past executive producer of *Laugh-In* and executive producer of the Comedy Awards. Jann was the person who coordinated the guests, the talent, seating, caterers, and everything else. She and I hit it off immediately because we both loved to trash-talk celebrities. She had lots of experience in the area as she was once personal assistant to Stephanie Powers, from *Hart to Hart*. She knew a ton of celebrities.

Because I didn't know a thing about LA and the show business pyramid scheme, meaning those at the bottom had a long way to go until they got to the top and collected the big bucks, I was humble about getting an invitation, along the lines of "I know this is very last minute," and "I hate to trouble you with this," and "If there's no room for me, I'll understand." Jann put me on the permanent list and I went every year until ABC stopped televising the event in 2001. Later in our friendship, Jann told me that many comedians tried bullying to get an invitation. "Don't you know who I am?" kind of bullying. None of them got invited.

No matter what it looks like on the outside, the real theme of Hollywood is to be nice. There's a long-forgotten story about Michael J. Fox, who was starring in the biggest sitcom of the day, *Family Ties*, and at the same time starring in the hit movie, *Back to the Future*. A reporter asked him if he considered himself the luckiest, most talented guy in Hollywood, and Fox replied, "No, I'm just the guy that's easiest to get along with."

Sidebar: After standing in for Betty White on *Love, Sidney*, my second stand-in job was for Michael J. Fox's wife, Tracy Pollan, on a Movie of the Week. I'm taller than she is but a blonde is a blonde is a blonde.

Each year I took a guest to the Awards. Free drinks, fabulous food, and a swag bag at the end of the night. I still have the jumper cables I got one year. I don't know how to use them but I have them, in case anyone else can. I should probably keep them in my car.

Sidebar: One year Lindy imported handmade bags from Brazil and was under consideration for that year's Oscar swag bag. When she found out she had to give them away for free she withdrew her name from the donator's list. I think her exact words were, "Are they fucking crazy?" This from a girl who sold cocaine to the Rolling Stones.

For many years Richard Pryor was a guest at the Awards. His Multiple Sclerosis had advanced by then and he was confined to a wheel chair, so he sat at a table down in front.

Each year I'd find a comedian in the room and ask them to go with me to Richard's table but they all turned me down. I was too big a chicken to go by myself. Pryor was the Godfather of Comedy.

Kim Coles, of the 1990s TV shows *In Living Color* and *Living Single,* was one of the people I tried to persuade to come with me. She and I had done stand-up together in NY, mostly at the Duplex, one of the comedy clubs that banned me.

Sidebar: Rick, the owner, was in prison doing time for drug possession. On stage one night I said I'd slept with him. Which I hadn't. I didn't know it but his wife was in the audience and believed me, subsequently banning me from the club. Fellow comedian Angela Scott offered to get a petition going to override the ban but I turned her down. I was afraid other comedians would get banned if they signed it. When Rick got out of prison, he apologized for his now ex-wife's behavior and invited me back to the club, but I was moving to Los Angeles the next day.

"Kim, come with me to Richard's table."
"Why?"
"I want to talk to him and I'm afraid to go by myself."
"Girl, that's RICHARD."
"Oh come *onnnnnnnnn*."
"Forget it Soro, you're on your own."

It was nice to know I wasn't the only one afraid to approach him. He had that effect on comics. No one could ever best Pryor at standup, only a few were even on his level. It was like he invented stand-up comedy all over again. So every year I sat through the awards and stared at Pryor's table like the obsessive - and troubled - individual that I am.

Then one year, tired of taking my deadbeat boyfriend, whose only goal was to look at celebrity cleavage, be first in line for the swag bag, and then storm the valet so we would miss the crowds, I took my sister. When I asked her to come meet Richard she agreed immediately. She had no fear of embarrassing herself in front of him because she knew I'd do that all by myself. Plus she'd been drinking.

Richard was listening to his wife and I thought she'd never stop talking. I stood behind him while my heart beat out of my chest. I didn't even know what I would say if he did acknowledge me. When she finally stopped talking I tapped him on the shoulder.

At the exact same time a photographer appeared at his table, lifted his camera and prepared to take his picture. When Richard turned to face me the photographer put his camera down. Apparently I'm only famous in my imagination.

"You're the reason I wanted to become a stand-up and I know you might think you inspired a generation of male comics but you inspired me too and you might think you inspired a generation of black comics but you inspired white comics too," I said without taking a breath.

And then my eyes filled with tears. Outside of crying in front of Angelina Jolie and any boyfriend that dumped me, I'm usually as dry as an alcoholic at an AA meeting. Richard said nothing. But he motioned to the photographer to take a photo of us both. I leaned down close to him and the photographer snapped about five pictures. I thanked Richard and walked away with Lindy. The photographer also walked away and I ran to catch up with him.

"I'm going to need that roll of film."
"Not possible, they belong to ABC plus there are plenty of other celebrities on the roll and I'm not giving those away. Sorry."
"You don't understand; that was Richard *Pryor*. My idol. I have to have a picture of us together."

The photographer was surprisingly sympathetic.

"Fine, I'll use another roll of film in my other camera. Let's go."

We walked back to Richard's table. I couldn't believe I was going to ask him to take another picture with me.

"The photographer couldn't give me the roll of film because it belonged to ABC but he got out a blank roll of film and said he would take another picture of us and I'm really sorry to do this to you but I really need to have a picture of us together that is if you don't mind and I'm really really sorry I'm being a pain in the ass." I was now sweating top-shelf vodka and again, not breathing.

Richard looked at the photographer and nodded for him to snap away. I thanked him, again, and trailed the photographer when he walked away, again. He rewound his camera and gave me the roll of film.

Not all paparazzi are evil. One percent can be swayed to the good side through the magic of exposed cocktail dress cleavage. So thanks for that, Lindy.

The encounter with Richard Pryor is one of the most treasured memories I have of my stand-up career. It erases the married comic who came into my room at 3:00 a.m. wearing only a towel. It erases the booker at Catch a Rising Star who kept telling me he didn't think I was funny. It erases being cheated out of my *Star Search* win in front of millions of people on national TV. Granted, I have a big mouth and am not shy by nature but if you don't have a big mouth, and you are shy, don't let an opportunity pass to tell someone you admire how much they mean to you. Even if they're famous. It will stay with you for the rest of your life.

Amazon review by SteelByContrary: 5.0 out of 5 stars
Brava to you as I would have been too scared to approach my idol, Justin Bieber.

Author Suzy Soro's reply to SteelByContrary:
You and me both.

I Would Never Do This Again But It's Too Late Anyway Because She's Dead

In 1985 I was at the Waldorf Astoria in New York City for the Friars Club roast of Mr. Television, Milton Berle, one of the first comedians to have his own show. Milton was known for two things: He was a notorious joke thief and legendary for the size of his penis. Had he lived longer in the Internet age, his dick would have gone viral more times than Gangnam Style.

I was at the roast with Mr. Y, a man I was dating who claimed to be a distant cousin of Milton's. I had no reason not to believe him although I never saw a copy of their family tree. Like other questions in relationships, "Where were you until 3 a.m.?" and "What do you mean she's your friend from work?" there are some answers you prefer not to hear unless you're medicated.

Mr. Y completed a documentary on Milton for the Museum of Broadcasting and the roast coincided with the release of the documentary. The dais had actors from stage and screen: Sammy Davis Jr., Maureen Stapleton, Tom Bosley, and Ruth Gordon, and every major comedian of that era: Dick Cavett, Red Buttons, Norm Crosby, Jan Murray, Abe Vigoda, Dick Shawn, Jackie Vernon and Henny Youngman. And the most famous comedian of them all, Lucille Ball.

Since I spent the majority of my youth watching reruns of *I Love Lucy*, I spent the majority of that roast watching Lucy. I was waiting for her to do something funny, evidently not having understood that the roast wasn't for her. She sat on the dais and did not do one funny thing. When she went to the podium to skewer Milton I don't remember any of her speech because in my joy over seeing her, I lost my hearing. One of the only things I remember from that night was that Barbara Walters was listed as part of the entertainment in the program. Baffling. Also, what the fuck?

When the roast was over, Mr. Y and I mingled briefly, found Milton to say our goodbyes, and then headed for the elevators. Milton was very nice to me, even complimented my dress. I never saw him again after that but according to Mr. Y, Milton was somewhat of a control freak, insisted on going over every frame of his documentary, every lighting cue, every shot. That's probably why he noticed my dress. He was detail-oriented.

On the way out I noticed something shiny and gold on the floor. It was a little plaque that was on the award the Friars gave Milton. It had his name, the date, and the Friars logo on it. I realized it had fallen off and my first thought was to return it to Milton. Obviously. My second thought was to keep it. Obviously.

I kept it. Obviously.

Mr. Y and I got to the elevators and as the door opened, the two people waiting ahead of us stepped inside. It was Lucille Ball and her husband Gary Morton. I looked at Mr. Y wide-eyed but he shook his head No. I gave him the Are You Fucking Kidding Me look and again he shook his head No.

As I stood there fuming I glanced at Lucy. She had backed into a corner and had her face down, staring at the fascinating floor of the elevator. Her husband was standing a few feet away and staring into space, like he'd never seen her before.

Lucy didn't want to be recognized. She didn't want to hear for the eighty-trillionth time that someone was her biggest fan. That someone once did the *Lucy Cry* at a New York audition for a Shakespearean production and unbelievably got a callback off that impersonation. That someone owned the entire Collector's Edition of *I Love Lucy* on VHS. VHS!

The most famous comedian in the world wanted her privacy so I kept my mouth shut. Would she have responded if I'd said hello? Would she have yelled at me to leave her alone? I'll never know.

And that's why, so many years later, I made sure I talked to Richard Pryor.

Amazon Review by HymenealAm: 2.0 out of 5 stars
I did not like her writing in this book. It wasn't that funny. I laughed maybe three times while reading the entire book. She was trying too hard with her jokes. It also showed me someone with a gargantuan ego who has a lot of false modesty.

Author Suzy Soro Reply to HymenealAm:
I knew I saw this review somewhere before. You copied it verbatim from one of Tina Fey's reviews on her book, Bossypants. I'm flattered.

The Fighter, The Director, The Comedian

When I lived in Paris for three years, after escaping a very bad relationship in San Francisco, I lived with my mother and Lindy. Mom worked Monday through Friday so after I went through all her things and stole from her private stash of money that was not that well hidden, I was usually bored with nothing to do. (This was right before the Rolling Stones came to town and before I was hired to lead a Can-Can.) I read in the *International Herald Tribune* that Muhammad Ali was coming to town for the French publication of his book, *The Greatest*. Thinking it was going to be a routine show and tell I went to the venue only to be told it was for press only.

"I'm with the press."

"You don't have a press badge."

"They forgot to give it to me."

"Who's they?"

"They, the press people."

"Who do you work for?"

"*The International Herald Tribune?*"

"They're already here."

"I know, they told me to meet them here."

"All right, go ahead. Pick up a copy of the book; they're on a table by the door."

Mumammad Ali and me at the book signing for *The Greatest*

I pushed past all the people until I was standing right next to Ali. Everyone else shouted at him in French and he smiled and ignored everyone.

"Hi, Mr. Ali."

"American?"

"Yes."

"Hmmm. Give me your book." I handed it to him and he signed it. "I'll tell you one thing; I don't know how you got in here but I know you're not press."

"How do you know?"

"Your clothes match."

***

One of my biggest supporters in LA was writer and director Michael Patrick King. I worked with him at the Improv in NY and ran into him in and out of the Hollywood Hills or at different venues over the years. One night, we were both at a party and a female comic sequestered me from the normal people and began a long treatise on iridology.

"It's the study of the human iris. An iridologist reads them and can tell your overall health from the reading."

"Do they read animal irises?"

"Of course." Add one more thing to the long list of why people hate Long Angeles.

"That can't be cheap."

"It isn't."

"Honey, I don't even have this month's rent so seeing an iridologist isn't going to be high on my list."

At that moment Michael walked by.

The next day he called and invited me to lunch. He was a successful writer by then, worked on *Murphy Brown* among other shows. At the end of lunch he handed me a check for a thousand dollars.

"For your rent."

"Michael, I can't, it's too much."

"I'm not taking it back. Keep it, you need it and I'm doing fine." He went on to direct *Sex and the City,* both the TV show and the two movies. Michael has always been successful. He doesn't eat sugar and if that's the reason he's successful in Hollywood, then I'm in big trouble.

He used to call me in to audition for shows he was working on. One in particular, *Good Advice*, starred Shelley Long, from *Cheers*. Shelley had a reputation in Hollywood as being difficult to work with, not because she wasn't a good actor, or a funny one, but because she was so exacting. She had trouble with wardrobe fittings because if something was a half an inch off her liking, she'd insist it be re-tailored. Rumor had it wardrobe was thrilled when Kirstie Alley replaced her, because she was fine with anything they put her in.

Michael was directing shows by then and had auditioned

me many times, but I never got any of the roles. They usually went to someone with a bigger resume, or to Wendie Malick, (*Hot in Cleveland, Just Shoot Me*) who I grew to fear if I saw her at an audition.

Michael Patrick King and me

Michael gave me a cold open on one of Shelley's episodes. The cold open is the short segment that opens a show, then there's a commercial, and then the actual episode airs. I was playing one of Shelley's psychiatric patients. I can hear you thinking "type casting" from here. I don't remember what the line was, but whatever it was, I had to do it over. And then they rewrote it and I had to do it again. Michael was fine with the final line but Shelley wasn't.

"Michael, what if she said the word The instead of An?"
"It's good the way it is."
"But wouldn't The make more sense in this scene?"

"Shelley, it's fine. Let it alone."
"I just think that if you look at it..."
"Shelley! Moving on!!"

That wasn't really the conversation they had but it was similar, over something small and inconsequential. Shelley Long was a huge star and I was shocked that Michael, my friend, my fellow comedian, had talked to her that way. And that's when I realized he'd moved way past where I had him in my head. He was the big boss.

And Shelley moved on.

The following year I saw her at The American Comedy awards and barged right into her conversation. I reminded her of the episode and scene I was in on *Good Advice* and she was so sweet. I mean really sweet. But then again, I wasn't in the wardrobe department of NBC.

***

George Carlin was playing in Vegas the same weekend I did my first gig there. Only he was in the big room at Bally's and I was at Catch a Rising Star, the smaller comedy club in the same casino. This Catch a Rising Star did not have the hateful little man booker who didn't think I was funny.

On a whim I left George a message at the front desk, said I was a comic, was playing there for the week, and was there any chance I could meet him? He called my room and asked if I was in a relationship, and when I said I was, offered me two tickets to his Valentine's Day show. But the guy I was dating was in LA and wasn't coming to Vegas to join me so I went to George's show by myself. I caught the first half before I had to leave and do my own show.

The next day the box office manager of Catch A Rising Star handed me a note from George. It said, "Wanted to know if you saw the show."

I'd forgotten to write him and tell him how funny he was. A BIG NO-NO IS NOT TELLING A COMEDIAN THEY'RE

FUNNY AFTER YOU'VE SEEN THEIR SHOW, especially when it's a very funny comedian like George Carlin. But that's not why he left me a message, to get a compliment. He left me that note to make sure I'd gotten in without a hassle. He wanted to make sure I'd had a good time. He was a genuinely kind man who loved comedians. And comedians loved him right back.

I wrote him a note.

And yes, he was very, very funny that night. And every other night he performed.

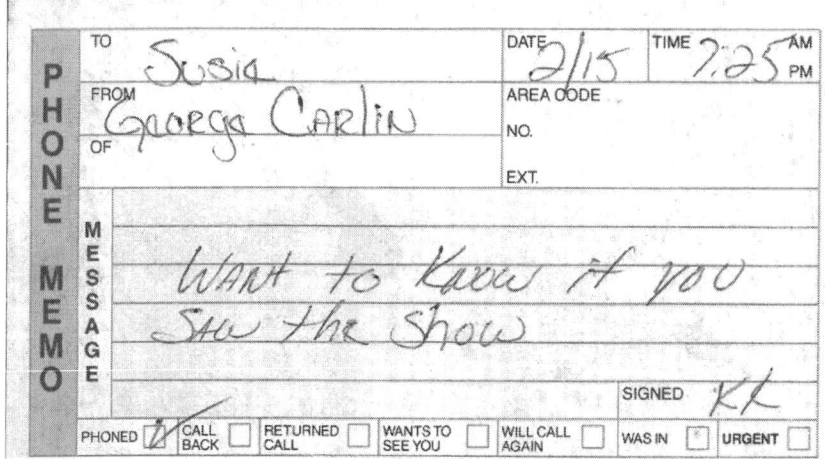

Amazon review from AmiableAndShocks: 5.0 out of 5 stars
I loved George Carlin. Glad to hear he was a nice man and that you helped keep his memory alive.

The Conclusion, the End or the Epilogue, Take Your Pick

    I can't figure out how to end this book. Like a relationship well past its expiration date, I sort of know but hang on like a ripe apple in heavy denial, unable to drop from a branch of the tree. I sway back and forth hoping a strong wind or a Freudian psychiatrist knocks me to the ground. And yes, I'm aware apples can't be in denial and don't go around thinking they're peaches. At least not the ones on Prozac.

    I didn't tell all the stories, like the one about goading Maggie Wheeler into talking to see if she sounded like her character on *Friends*, Janice. She doesn't. Or the one about going to lunch with comedian Jackie Mason, and staring so hard at the pancake makeup on his face I didn't remember one piece of advice he gave me about comedy. *And then agreed to go out with him again.* Or the one about meeting fugitive director Roman Polanski in a Paris nightclub, and then going to his house to drink wine and take Quaaludes. Or the one about meeting Erik Estrada from *C.H.I.P.S.* at a party in Beverly Hills and being shocked because he was absolutely hilarious.

    So I'll conclude with the story about who I think made me unable to have closure with anyone and anything: My parents.

Sidebar: You can't mention Freud and then not blame your parents. It's the law.

Each night when I was growing up, I'd lie in bed in my upstairs bedroom, waiting for the nighttime ritual of my parents tucking me in and saying goodnight. Making sure I'd recited the dreadful prayer, *If I should die before I wake*, because why not end your day on an up note? I'd lie there, my arms draped haphazardly in the sheets and blankets on my twin bed. Dad came upstairs first. He'd pick up the sheets and blankets and physically put my arms over them. Then he'd shove the covers under the edges of the mattress until I was swaddled by my own bed. Then my mother came up afterwards and loosened the sheets and blankets and pulled them up to my chin, where I had no other choice but to keep my arms inside the covers. Then she would take the covers and shove them under the edges of the mattress until I was once again swaddled by my own bed. A blonde burrito.

They repeated this ritual every night until I turned thirty, or is that only the recurring nightmare I have once a month? No deviation whatsoever, unless Mom came upstairs before Dad and the whole process was reversed. In all that time, neither of them noticed what the other parent did. Mom never noticed that by the time she arrived, I was on my back, arms akimbo. And if Dad came up after her, he never noticed the mummified state she'd left me in. Nor was it ever taken into account how I'd placed my arms before the first parent even arrived. *The way I wanted.*

So I blame them for my inability to end something in a decisive fashion. Because I'm waiting for someone else to show up after it has ended, and do it another way.

Amazon review by: ZooSyrus 100.0 out of 100 stars
I liked this book a lot. I tried to download the Kindle version but forgot I don't have a Kindle. This would make a great gift for an obsessive-compulsive who has boundary issues and loves show business gossip. It's funny and bitchy and yes, I wrote this review.

~ *Suzy Soro, my close friends call me Suji*

P.S. Dear Ryan Gosling, I'd like to apologize in advance for whatever stupid thing I will say or do when I finally meet you. I'll probably try and make you laugh. (It's a sickness.)

This is not simply a dishy memoir about stars. Soro knows how to deliver pathos with deadpan, self-deprecating humor. Basically, she's really funny, and you will relate to every self-conscious, star-struck, or hilarious moment.

~ Jess Riley, anxious author of *Driving Sideways* and *All the Lonely People*

****

Darkly funny, unabashedly honest, and voyeuristic with every word, Celebrity sTalker will be relished by anyone on the other side of the red carpet.

~ Adam Heath Avitable, comedian and author of *Interviews with Dead Celebrities*

****

See how Suzy Soro parlayed her chance meeting with one of America's biggest celebrities into a hilarious and embarrassing anecdote that she clearly has not gotten over yet.

~Caissie St. Onge, former assistant to David Letterman, former writer for Rosie O'Donnell and producer of Bravo's *Watch What Happens Live!* Author of *Jane Jones, Worst. Vampire. Ever.*

****

"I once saw Morgan Freeman in an elevator and screamed at the top of my lungs. I bet Suzy would have pushed the Emergency Stop button. Her painstakingly funny book CELEBRITY sTALKER, in which she accounts her brushes with fame, is riveting and entertaining."

~Comedian Wendy Liebman, Letterman, Leno, Fallon and Carson (Johnny, not Daly.)

To Suzy Soro, Hollywood is one big mixer, and she's determined to work the room whether it likes it or not. Suzy's approach to celebrity is a revelation. Cataloging her catch-and-release encounters with some of the biggest names in Hollywood, Celebrity sTalker gives readers a hilarious and subversive view of life in the real Tinsel Town from a comedian who has lived it both inside...and out.

~ Anna Lefler, comedian and author of *THE CHICKTIONARY: FROM A-LINE TO Z-SNAP, THE WORDS EVERY WOMAN SHOULD KNOW*

Printed in Great Britain
by Amazon.co.uk, Ltd.,
Marston Gate.